The Book of
STITHIANS

The Changing Face of a Cornish Parish

HALSGROVE

First published in Great Britain in 1999

Copyright © 1999 Stithians Parish History Group

Dedication
The authors dedicate their joint contributions to the memory
of the late Basil Green, to all Stithians people past and present, as
well as to those who made the supreme sacrifice in both world wars.
They gave their tomorrow that we may have our today.
May light perpetual shine.

---

*All rights reserved. No part of this publication may be reproduced,
stored in a retrieval system, or transmitted in any form or by any means
without the prior permission of the copyright holder.*

British Library Cataloguing-in-Publication Data
A CIP record for this title is available from the British Library

ISBN 1 84114 043 0

HALSGROVE
PUBLISHING, MEDIA AND DISTRIBUTION

Halsgrove House
Lower Moor Way
Tiverton, Devon EX16 6SS
Tel: 01884 243242
Fax: 01884 243325
website: http://www.halsgrove.com

Printed and bound in Great Britain by Bookcraft Ltd., Midsomer Norton

Contents

Foreword by F. Julian Williams, CBE, MA   4
Acknowledgements   5
Introduction by Tony Langford   7

CHAPTER 1:   CORNISH CROSSES (TL)   9
CHAPTER 2:   PRINCIPAL PROPERTIES (JI/TL)   11
CHAPTER 3:   TRANSPORT (JG)   19
CHAPTER 4:   ST STYTHIANS PARISH CHURCH (AP)   23
CHAPTER 5:   METHODISM (JG)   29
CHAPTER 6:   AGRICULTURE (JG)   37
CHAPTER 7:   SCHOOL DAYS (AP)   45
CHAPTER 8:   ST STITHIANS COLLEGE (JI)   61
CHAPTER 9:   IN TIMES OF WAR (AP/JI)   65
CHAPTER 10: QUARRYING (JI)   73
CHAPTER 11: CSM GEOTHERMAL ENERGY PROJECT (AP)   81
CHAPTER 12: KENNALL VALE (JI)   83
CHAPTER 13: MINING (JI)   91
CHAPTER 14: STITHIANS RESERVOIR (AP)   95
CHAPTER 15: SOME OF THE MANY RENOWNED STITHIANS FOLK (JG/AP)   101
CHAPTER 16: GROUPS AND ORGANISATIONS (JG/JI)   113
CHAPTER 17: SPORT AND ENTERTAINMENT (JI/TL)   127
CHAPTER 18: VIEWS OF STITHIANS OLD AND NEW (JG)   137

Sources   156
Subscribers   157

*Individual authors are referred to as follows: Alison Penaluna, AP;
Joyce Green, JG; Janet C.M. Ivey, JI; Tony Langford, TL.*

Foreword

It is a great honour to write a foreword for *The Book of Stithians* and I congratulate Alison Penaluna and her team for their achievement in producing this volume which has taken such devoted and sustained effort over the last 25 years.

Nothing stands still, but it is the pace of modern life that is so amazing. The past century has seen the rate of change accelerate more than ever, to the point where it has become hard to keep up, and with further surprises in store as the power of the computer becomes increasingly pronounced. This book gives us a chance to look back at the Stithians of bygone, calmer times, in an era, for example, when the fact that 'buses go daily to Falmouth and Redruth and on Wednesdays to Truro' was something to write home about!

So congratulations once again to all who have produced this very valuable and interesting volume and may it succeed in illuminating the recent history of an historic Cornish parish.

F. Julian Williams
Caerhays Castle, Gorran

A once familiar sight, milk churns at the end of the lane.

Acknowledgements

This impressive collection of photographs springs from two substantial collections; the first, commenced by the late Basil Green (former member of the Stithians Parish History Group) and now used here by his wife Mrs Joyce A. Green, the second, belonging to Mrs Alison Penaluna. Mrs Green therefore dedicates her collection to the memory of her late husband and Mrs Penaluna dedicates her collection to Stithians people everywhere. It was when these members realised just how many photographs they possessed that the idea for this book was born. However, *The Book of Stithians* would not have been possible without the help of a great many people connected to the parish and beyond who have lent material, searched for names and aided research in so many different ways. The Stithians Parish History Group would like to thank them one and all:

Mrs Christine Barnicoat, Mr Tony Bayfield, Mr R. Beale, Mrs Beth Berriman, Mr Eric Berry, Dr C.A. Biscoe, Ruth Berriman, Mr Jack Berriman, Miss Angela Broome, Mrs Marlene Brush, Mrs Veronica Chesher, Mrs Valerie Collins, Mrs Kim Cooper, Jane Corey (formerly of Carncrees Farm), the late Mr G.D. Corey (formerly of Carncrees Farm), Mr and Mrs M. Couldrey, J. Arthur Dixon, Mrs Elizabeth Downing, Mrs Marian Downing, Mrs D. Dunstan, Christopher D. Dunstan, Miss Helen Dunstan, Mrs Kathleen Dunstan, Mr Reggie Dunstan, Mr Leonard Evans, Mrs Nancy Evans, Mrs Rosemary Evans, Mrs Louie Ford, Miss Janet Gluyas, Mrs Olive Gluyas, Mrs S. Gough (Clerk, Stithians Parish Council), Mrs Joyce Green, the late F.L. Harris, Mrs G. Hay, Miss B. Hegarty, M. Henning, Ms J. Hillman, Mr Keith Holloway, Mrs E. Hopper, Mr James Carol Ivey, Miss M. Jellie, Mr and Mrs R. Jolly, Mr D. Kitto (Clerk, Penryn Town Council), Mr G. Knight, Mr Christopher Knuckey, Mr John R. Knuckey, the late Mr Peter Knuckey, Mr Arthur Langford, Mrs Glencoe Langford, Mr Roger Langford, Mr and Mrs A. Martin, Mr Bernard Martin, Mrs Kathleen Martin, Mr Edward A. Martin, Miss Janie Moore, Verne O'Brien (Northern Territory, Australia), Mrs Marilyn O'Neil (Office Manager, CSM Associates Ltd.), the late Mr J.L. Odgers and Mrs Leila Odgers, Mr Oliver Padel, Mrs Amy Pascoe, Mrs Lorna Pascoe, Mrs Molly Pascoe, Mrs Margery Pascoe, Mr Mervyn Pascoe, Mrs Peggy S. Pascoe, Mr Roy Pascoe, Mr Tom Penaluna, Mr R.D. Penhallurick, Mr and Mrs E. Penlerick, Mr Dominick Penrose, Mr Edward Perry, Mr Ivan Perry, the late Mr Oscar Peters, Mr William Prowse, Mr N. Pryor, Mrs Eleanore Rashleigh, Mrs Fay Richards, Dr M.J. Ripley, the late Edwin John Sarah, Mr Hugh Scanlon, Mr J.N. Seth, Mr H.A. Smith, John R. Smith, Mrs Elaine Tangye, Mr Thomas, Professor Charles Thomas, CBE, DL, Mrs Yvonne Toms, the late Mr R. Toy (formerly of Carnvullock Farm), Mr L. Tresidder, Mrs Carrie Veall, Mrs Joy Walker, the late Mr J.R. Williams, Mr Leonard Williams, Mrs Marion Williams, Mrs Mary C. Williams, Mr Ross Williams, Mr Trevor Wills, Mr David Wylde (rector and headmaster of St Stithians College), the late Mr Kitchener Young (Mabe and formerly of Stithians).

Thanks also to the following bodies, institutions and publications (past and present): Air Historical Branch (RAF of the Ministry of Defence, London), Bailey-Howe Library, Vermont, USA, Birmingham Public Library (Reference Library Department), the British Library, Justin Brooke (Affiliate IMM), Bunyup Press (Gawler, Southern Australia), *Cornubian and Redruth Times*, Cornwall Archaeology Unit, Cornwall Record Office, Cornish Studies Library (Redruth), Courtney Library, Cornwall Trust for Nature Conservation, CSM Associates Ltd., Devon Record Office, *Express and Echo*, Hampshire County Council Local Studies Collection, *Falmouth Packet*, Falmouth Town Council (the Clerk), Halsgrove (Simon Butler, Denise Lyons and Naomi Cudmore), Historical Society (Southern Australia), James Martin Museum (Willaston, Southern Australia), Kerrier District Council Planning Department, Master's Office of the Supreme Court (South Africa), National Monuments Council, the National Trust (for use of the Lanhydrock Atlas), Public Record Office (Southern Australia), *Redruth Independent Newspaper*, South Africa, Royal Cornwall Polytechnic Society, Royal Institution of Cornwall, Society of Genealogists, London, South Australia Archives, South West Water (Exeter and Truro), St Stithians College Library, Stithians Ladies Choir, Stithians Parish Council, Stithians County Primary School, St Stythians Male Voice Choir, Messrs E.F.K. Tucker, Nupen and Goodman (Johannesburg), the War Graves Division (South Africa), *West Briton*, *Western Independent*, *Western Morning News*.

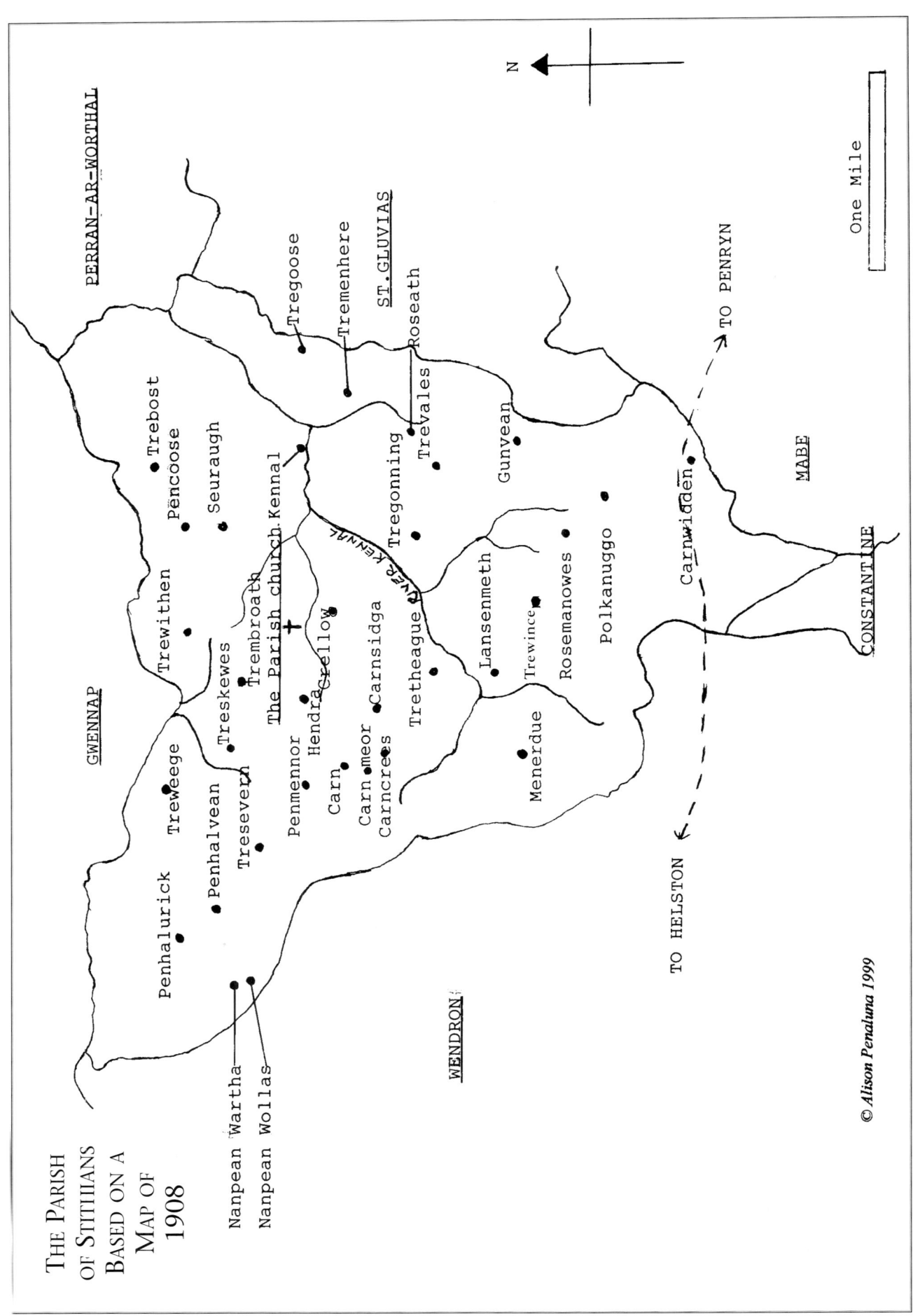

INTRODUCTION

Stithians is a rural parish about five miles south of Redruth and derives its name from the patron saint, about whom little is known. In 1268, the patron saint was recorded as Sancta Stethyana and in 1524 as Stethyans. In the intervening period there were several variations, including Sancta Stediana, Seint Stethyent, St Stidianus and Seynt Stedyan – and it is also unclear as to whether this mysterious figure was a man or a woman.

When the first government census was taken in 1801, the population of Stithians stood at 1269. It then rose, reaching a peak of 2530 at the time of the 1841 census. This was largely due to the development of copper mining in neighbouring parishes. After 1841 the population began to decline and in 1961 stood at 1290 – virtually the same figure as reached 160 years earlier. The 1971 census showed a reversal in this trend with a figure of 1435, and by 1981 the population stood at 2140. This was chiefly due to major building development, which itself was largely triggered by the provision, in 1971, of a sewerage system for the village and a reservoir catchment area. The population at the time of writing stands at 2070.

Stithians Impounding Reservoir (officially opened in October 1967) has become a well-known feature of the local landscape. Covering 274 acres (111 hectares), it is a popular centre for fishing and water sports. It is also an important haven for birds and attracts birdwatchers from all over the country. The Cornwall Bird-Watching and Preservation Society manages part of the reservoir as a reserve and has two observation hides. The highlight of the year in the parish is Stithians Show. From small beginnings in 1834 it has become what is probably the biggest and best one-day agricultural show in the country.

Because of its relative isolation Stithians has always had to make its own entertainment and this continues to this day with the current *Stithians Directory* listing no less than 55 organisations in the parish. It even has its own bi-monthly publication, the *Stithians Times*, produced by a small team from the Village Hall Committee. At a time when we hear so much of rural decline it is pleasing to note that the parish of Stithians remains vibrant.

Tony Langford
1999

In 1992 Stithians Show purchased 65 acres of Kennall Farm as the event was growing and a permanant site was needed (courtesy of Culdrose RNAS).

Clockwise from top: *The cross standing in a field on Trevales Farm (Trevales Cross No. 1). Depicted in relief on the face shown is a cross, the lower limb of which extends to the base of the shaft; the cross in the churchyard, formerly located at Seaureaugh Mill, on this face of which the figure of Christ is depicted in relief; the cross in the grounds of the Old Vicarage Hotel. Charles Henderson describes it as 'a late example of a round-headed cross, with chamfered edges'; the late Mr Basil Green admiring the cross in the grounds of Trevales House (Trevales Cross No. 2); the cross at Tretheague, both faces of which have an equal-limbed cross with a bead in relief.*

Chapter 1: Cornish Crosses

Several of the crosses in the parish of Stithians are not in their original locations. The cross in the grounds of the Old Vicarage Hotel (formerly the Vicarage) was found buried in the churchyard, though the date of its discovery does not appear to have been recorded. The cross currently in the churchyard was formerly located at Seaureaugh Mill, which is where A.G. Langdon saw it. In his book *Old Cornish Crosses* (1896) he records: 'The cross stands in the garden, near the stream'.

The cross now standing in a corner of a field approximately 100 metres south east of Tretheague House was found by a monumental mason in 1921, lying on the bed of the River Kennall. A manuscript in the County Museum, Truro, by Baird and White ('Cornish Crosses', 1960) specifies that it was found beneath the north arch of Tretheague Bridge and that it was thought to have stood originally on a small island by the bridge. At the spring meeting of the Royal Institution of Cornwall in 1921 the Revd R.F. Moody, MA, exhibited a photograph of the cross. Permission to remove it from the stream and re-erect it was granted by Mr J.C. Williams of Caerhays Castle, the then owner of Tretheague. Mr Williams also offered to pay for the operation. The cross was recorded as being 4 feet 10 inches high, 16 inches wide, and 9 inches thick.

The cross that now stands in the grounds of Trevales House once stood at Hendra. A.G. Langdon gave the original location of this cross (described as 'Trevales Cross No. 2') as being on Hendra Hill 'at a point on the south side of the road almost opposite Stythians Wesley Meeting House'. It was moved to Trevales in c.1860 by Mr Moore, the owner of the Trevales and Hendra Estates. Curiously it was not re-fixed in the base at Trevales but sunk into the ground alongside it.

At the head of this stone on this face there there is a cross depicted in relief.

A Stithians bootmaker, William Henry Gluyas, put pen to paper and recorded his memories of the cross and his disapproval of its removal from the Hendra site in verse. His poem appeared in the *Cornubian* on 8 September 1910:

An Old Cornish Cross

I do remember very well,
Just at the foot of Hendra Hill,
A cross stood out all hoar with age.

That cross that stood at Hendra's Hill
Was covered o'er with moss; and still
I have remembrance of the spot
It occupied and not a jot
Or tittle of the scene has passed.
It was a heavy stone, and stood
Fixed firmly by the traveller's road,
Just a few feet on Hendra's side.
On it a form extended wide,
Represented Christ, the Lord.

The youth, the old, the rent, the grey,
When passing, would some moments stay.
There was a little trough below,
Placed firmly so that you could go
And wash you in the water pure,
And from some evil find a cure.
Wash some unseemly growth away,
And nine time drive disease away.
This little trough held water pure
And foul diseases it would cure.
And the coy youth would come betimes,
And plunge the hand in the nine times,
And then the wart would disappear
And the smooth skin again appear.

This is a reminiscence, O,
Of nearly fifty years ago.
That stone and trough were soon removed,
And taken to Trevales wood.
They never should have been removed.

W.H.G., Stithians

Unlike the Crellow House of the era pictured here, the property is now divided into four dwellings and two bungalows stand in part of the orchard. Some things have not changed, however; on Christmas Day St Stythians Band still proceeds up the drive to play carols in front of the house.

*Stithians Tennis Club at Crellow where they used the tennis court.
Left to right, back: L. Berryman, C. Dunstan, K. Holman, D. Trerise, V. Pascoe, H. Phillips, B. Henderson, C. Rowe, H. Mitchell, L. Mitchell, Revd W. Hills, W. Andrew;
middle: Mrs Simmons, E. Jelbert, S. Porter, R. Martin, P. Mitchell, O. Bowden;
front: P. Knuckey, E. Temby, M. Mitchell.*

Chapter 2: Principal Properties

CRELLOW HOUSE

Once the church town and largest village in the parish, Crellow is today part of Stithians village, although the name is still in evidence (Crellow Hill and Crellow Lane). The earliest reference to Crellow dates back to 1356, where it appears as 'Carellou'. It contains the element 'ker' which means 'fort' or 'round' and suggests the site of a round or enclosed settlement dating from the Iron Age/Romano-British period, 600BC to AD410.

As the original deeds of Crellow House have been lost, the precise date of its building is not known but the listed building description of the house dates it as early to mid 19th century. It seems probable that Crellow House was built for Captain James Martin (1772-1850), in the mid 1830s, just before he left Ennis and Carbis, a property on which he relinquished the lease at the end of 1836. He certainly appears as the owner/occupier of Crellow House at the time of the 1840 Tithe Apportionment which also shows him as the owner of three farms in the parish – Penhalvean East, Roseath and Trebarveth – all occupied by various members of his family.

James Martin was clearly a man of immense energy and wide-ranging talents. Indeed, he is listed variously as yeoman, butcher and innkeeper (which included keeping the Seven Stars). He is also shown as a mine agent, in which employment he worked for 50 years. It was, apparently, common practice to combine the roles of mine agent and innkeeper, for several such agents are recorded as running inns as a sideline.

One of the major houses of the parish, Crellow has played an important role in the social and community life of Stithians. A report in the *Penryn Advertiser* of 30 August 1907 reads:

Crellow House and farm... has recently been purchased by Mr B.C. Simmons by private treaty. The property comprises a charming residence, surrounded by beautifully wooded grounds, situated in one of the most picturesque parts of Cornwall, and altogether forms an ideal country seat.

A butcher by trade, Mr Ben Simmons had set up in business at Goonlaze and travelled around the nearby villages with his horse and wagon. He later helped to found the Red Car Motor Company, an enterprise with four large charabancs which took passengers to local towns and venues.

The Simmons era at Crellow House is well remembered by Miss Janie Moore, who was born in a cottage at Crellow in 1912 and has lived in Stithians all her life, a village of which she is fiercely proud. Her father, Mr Horace Moore, was employed by Mr Ben Simmons as a general factotum, his duties including those of gardener, butcher and farm labourer as well as helping on the buses. Miss Moore vividly recalls playing in the 'lovely grounds' and tells of the large lawns and many shrubs, including azaleas, camellias and rhododendrons. In the orchard were medlars and pears, while the greenhouse had 'peaches, vines and other plants'. She often helped Mrs Simmons to water the plants in the conservatory which held a lemon tree, roses, nectarines and a vine.

Not surprisingly, the grounds of Crellow House were a popular venue for garden fêtes, and chapel tea treats included Crellow on their processions around the village. For many years the British and Foreign Bible Society used Crellow as the venue for a fund-raising event. Each year an official from the BFBS would visit Stithians and those in the parish with collecting boxes would take them to Crellow House where they would have tea with the official and members of the Simmons family. This would be followed by an evening meeting at one of the Methodist chapels.

Hospital Sunday, an important fund-raising day for local hospitals, was also once held in the Crellow grounds. The *Penryn Advertiser* of 23 August 1912 carried a report of one such event:

A procession, headed by Helston Town Band, proceeded through the village to the beautiful grounds of Mr B.C. Simmons, Crellow House, where a service was presided over by Rev. W. Chambre Vaughan (Walsall). Addresses were given by the chairman, Revs. John I. Perry (Wesleyan), A.R. Martin (United Methodist), and Mr Charles T. Beard (Wesleyan), Perranwell. The band accompanied the singing.

In the evening the band gave an open air concert at Crellow House, under the baton of Bandmaster, W.A. Harris. The total receipts amounted to £31, the highest amount for several years.

During the Second World War Crellow House was to take on another role, that of a hostel for evacuees from London. For those children who could not be placed with families in the parish it was a permanent home. It also served as a sick bay where those who lived with families could go to be tended when they fell ill.

KENNALL VALE HOUSE

In the 14th century, the Kennall Estate and hamlet belonged to Roger de Carminow who died in 1308. Subsequently the manor passed to the Arundell family of Lanherne in St Mawgan in Pydar; Sir John Arundell inherited the lands on the death of his cousin, Joanna Carminow, in 1394, and the Arundell connection continued into the 1800s when ownership passed to the Bath brothers.

Kennall Vale House is situated on Kennall Manor land, about one mile east of the Parish Church. Established in a sequestered position and approached by a long tree-lined drive, the property is set in its own valley overlooking mature woodland and adjacent to the beautiful Kennall River (whose industrial past is of ongoing fascination to archaeologists and conservationists alike).

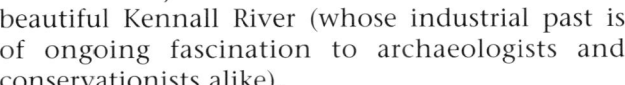
Kennall Vale House, c.1900, and from the side, c.1975 (below).

The substantial stone-built house is said to be of early Georgian origin and it is listed by the Department of the Environment as Grade II*. It has been described as one of the finest small mansion houses in West Cornwall and is indeed a rare example, retaining many original features both inside and out. Externally the house has appealing proportions, with a parapet at roof level and a string course at the level of the first floor. There are bow windows and decorative niches too. Internally the original mahogany doors and window shutters remain. Period touches add to the atmosphere of this delightful property with marble fireplaces, traditional deep skirtings, a vaulted ceiling in the entrance hall, as well as fine plasterwork on cornices and ceilings.

The tithe records of 1840 show the then landowner and occupant to be one William Tucker. At this time the property comprised over 38 acres including the renowned and substantial mill. The mansion was surrounded by its own land, identified as Tremenhere Field and Moor, Little Meadow, Homefield, Outer and Wood Fields, the Mowhay and Pond Moor, plus various waste and wet areas. Of particular note are the Double Field and Plantation, comprising two fields plus a central section of trees and recognised today as the plantation of tall trees, surrounded by a lake on the ground below the slope in front of Little Plymouth Cottages.

Other homesteads were included in the 1840 Tithe Apportionment; one was the locally familiar cottage found to the left of the road and entrance to the former offices of Messrs Polkinhorn and Company. The cottage was used as a store for many years and became dilapidated until recent years when it was restored once again to a charming dwelling, in harmony with the surroundings.

Kennall Vale Cottage was recorded also, to the right of the drive to Kennall Vale House and it remains there still. The tithe also lists all of the buildings at Little Plymouth and a further two homesteads with plantations along the north side of the valley in the direction of Ponsanooth. The first possessed an area of water, waste land and a plantation, on a site totalling around two acres. The second was located behind the Old Mill and covered an area of 11 perches. A third plantation, of some five acres, stood on the southern bank well down the valley and behind the mill, whilst a fourth – Poor Plantation – was positioned to the right of the roadway on the Stithians' side, just before the magnificent Kennall Bridge.

Edward David Polkinhorn was born in Perran-ar-Worthal in c.1850 and he once worked in a mill in the Bissoe Valley. He later secured the Kennall Mills, a decision that was to provide his family with security and parishioners with welcome employment. An exceptional record of employment with the Polkinhorn family was held by Norman Penaluna who worked there for over 50 years.

As the years passed, David Polkinhorn set up home in the valley with his wife, Lavinia, and their children, who were all born at Perranwell during the period 1874-77. The eldest was Edgar, followed by Ada and Samuel. David became the tenant of Kennall Vale House and in the early 1900s the property was in the ownership of the well-respected founders of the milling business which prospered by the side of the river. Edgar Polkinhorn succeeded his father and the Polkinhorn association continued until the late 1980s when the widowed Judy Polkinhorn (a much-loved lady) decided, sadly, that it was time for her and her son David to leave.

TRETHEAGUE HOUSE

J.E.B. Gover, in *The Place Names of Cornwall*, 1948, states that the settlement of Tretheague in the parish of Stithians is first recorded in 1213. The element 'Tre' implies a settlement of early medieval origin and it is interesting to note that Tretheague is marked as 'on site of Barton' on the 1893 Ordnance Survey Map, though the Ordnance Survey could find no trace of an earlier building.

Tretheague was one of the four major manors associated with Stithians, the others being Arworthal, Kennall and Penryn Corffe. The Manor of Tretheague claimed land at Carnmeor, Carnvean, Carnsidga, Crellow, Penhalvean, Penhalveor, Penmennor, Rosemanowes, Tregonning, Trembroath, Tresevern, Treskewes, Trewince and Vellandrucia.

In the 16th century Tretheague was held by the Beville family of Killygarth in Talland, passing by marriage to the Grenvilles of Stowe in the early 17th century. (The Bevilles descended from the De Beville who accompanied William the Conqueror in 1066 and was made a knight and placed as an officer at Truro.). It is possible that during their time as lords of the manor the Bevilles sold off parts of Tretheague, and it is highly likely that the Grenvilles spilt the manor up in the 17th century. It is known that Sir Bernard Grenville sold Penhalveor, one of the tenements, in 1620.

Writing in 1817, the historian, C.S. Gilbert, described Tretheague House as 'a good family mansion, sheltered by a cluster of ancient trees'. An observer today could well pen a similar description for it appears to have changed very little.

Tretheague House is a Grade II* listed building. A two-storey house over a basement, and with attics, it has a rusticated granite ashlar front while the remainder of the building is of granite rubble with granite and brick dressings. It has a dry delabole-slate hipped roof behind embattle parapet. The battlements are 20th century, having been added in the 1960s.

The house has a symmetrical, five-window east-north-east front with a central doorway which is approached by a flight of granite steps with (probably the original) wrought-iron railings. The doorway has a Gibbs surround and 'original panelled door with integral blind fanlight' (now glazed). The windows are mostly original 12-pane hornless sashes with wide glazing bars and 'much original crown glass'. The back of the house has its original doors and several original windows, including the fanlight head to the stair window. The principal rear doorway is approached by a granite bridge.

Tretheague House, 1999.

Behind the house is a walled garden with a retaining wall at the front, forming a passage between the garden and the basement of the house. Built into this retaining wall is a large ice house, which has a chamfered granite doorway and an entrance to a covered well. Adjoining the outside of the right-hand wall of the garden is a rectangular rubble closet with a slate roof. The closet was originally cleaned by a leat.

The interior of the house is fascinating, being virtually unaltered throughout since the 18th century. The listed building description draws attention to its many fine rococo ceilings and good quality 18th-century features, including chimney-pieces, panelled door architraves and some panelled walls with fielded panelling. The entrance hall has a fine plaster ceiling with modillions in the cornice. The stair hall, located at the rear of the house, has an 'open-well, open-string stair with three turned balusters per tread and a ramped handrail wreathed over the newel'. There is 'bolection moulding to the wall panels and under the landing'. There are two panels 'with eared architrave and scrolled pediments', and the plaster ceiling over the stair has 'dentils and modillions to the cornice and good quality rococo ceiling to the central panel'. The house has a basement kitchen and wine cellars with brick barrel vaults.

It is not possible to give an exact date for the building of the house as most of the deeds and other documents relating to Tretheague have been lost. John Bonython and Edward Martin have carried out independent research in recent years and both have come to the conclusion that Tretheague House was probably built in the early 1740s by Mr John Pearce. The architectural historian, Eric Berry, also puts the house at about 1740.

John Pearce had inherited Tretheague in 1741 on the death of his grandfather, Nicholas Pearce, who died aged 103. Nicholas Pearce, who had made a fortune out of mining in a neighbouring parish, acquired Tretheague in the 1690s. It seems that the previous owners, the Morton family, fell on misfortune. Writing in c.1710, the historian Thomas Tonkin claimed that the Mortons were 'oddly outed' from Tretheague by Nicholas Pearce. It is probable that they lost Tretheague through a default on a mortgage.

Despite being, in the words of Edward Martin, 'of doubtful literacy', Nicholas Pearce had risen to prominence. A clear indication of the Pearces' rise in the social scale was the marriage of Nicholas' eldest son, also called Nicholas, to Thomasine Trewren of Constantine on 18 December 1714. Thomasine was a member of an established local family of note and, more significantly, a granddaughter of Sir Richard Vyvyan of Trelowarren, a prominent member of county society. Nicholas junr pre-deceased his father, dying in March 1724, and Thomasine died three years later.

John Pearce had the distinction of being Sheriff of Cornwall in 1745, a more onerous task than in the present day. John also added to the Tretheague landholding by purchasing Penhalveor West from John Martin on 9 May 1755.

One of the clues as to the age of Tretheague House is the rococo-style plasterwork which puts it somewhere between 1720 and 1760. Edward Martin was able to narrow the date down further when he noticed similarities, in both plasterwork and other features, between Tretheague and other houses. These were Carelew (destroyed by fire on 5 April 1934) and the Mansion House and Prince's House in Truro, all of which were designed by Thomas Edwards of

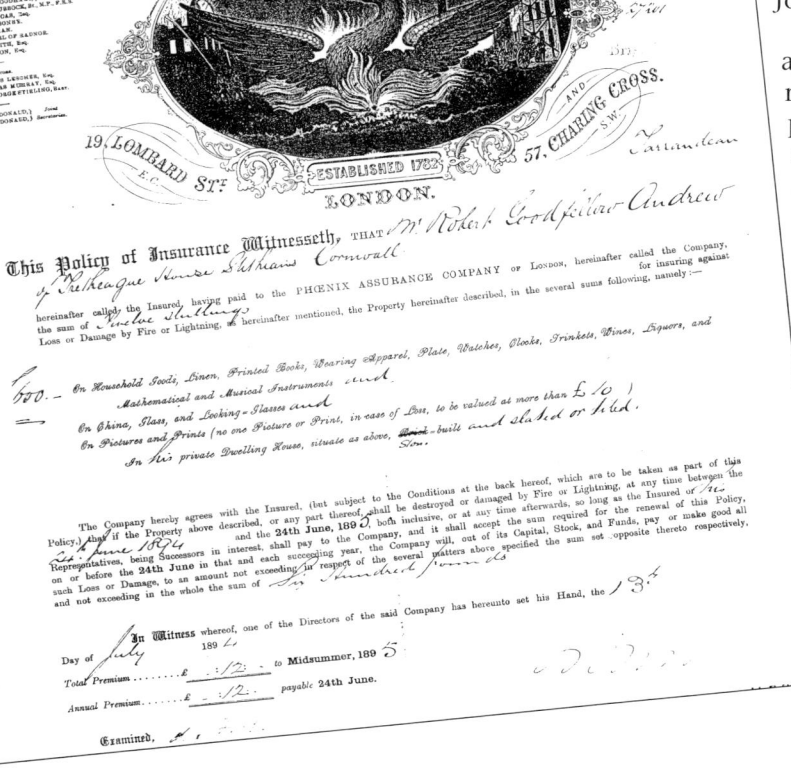

Left: *This policy of 13 July 1894, shows that Tretheague House and contents were insured for £600 at a premium of 12 shillings.*

Greenwich. In the case of Carelew, Edwards was involved when the house was altered and enlarged for William Lemon shortly after 1749. Prince's House was built in 1737 and the Mansion House between 1755 and 1762.

Comparisons have also been made between the interior of Tretheague and Trewardreva at Constantine where it is thought that Thomas Edwards did some interior work. These houses have similar staircases and plasterwork. Trewardreva belonged to the Trewren family into which, as previously mentioned, Nicholas Pearce junr had married.

It seems likely that Thomas Edwards was commissioned to design Tretheague House by John Pearce. When he inherited Tretheague (and a fortune) in 1741, John Pearce was a young man of 22 who moved in county circles. On 12 December 1744 John Pearce sold Ennis and Carbis, a farm in Stithians, to Walter Reed. On the sale document John Pearce was said to be 'of Trelissick'. Edward Martin has suggested he may have been living at Trelissick while Tretheague was being built.

Tretheague has always been a family home, sometimes lived in by its owners, often by tenants. It lends itself to big family occasions. When Winifred Andrew, the daughter of tenants Robert and Emily Andrew, married Hender Rowe on 21 October 1913 the reception was held at Tretheague House, and the grounds have long been sought after as a venue for parish events. St Stythians Silver Band held garden fêtes there for many years and one such was reported in the *Penryn Advertiser* on 31 August 1934:

Stythians Silver Band held its sixth annual fête on Saturday, in the beautiful grounds of Tretheague House, by permission of Mr W. Andrew. The weather was all that could be desired, and a good company was present at the opening ceremony, performed by Mrs W.W. Buckley (Trevales).

During the Second World War Tretheague House was not inhabited. Prior to the Normandy landings it was nearly taken over by the Americans, and the local Home Guard used it for a mock raid.

Today Tretheague is under the sympathetic ownership of Mr Dominick Penrose, who lives in the house with his wife, Nicky, and their children.

A fête at Tretheague in 1929. Note there are no battlements as these were added in 1969.

Trevales

The settlement of Trevales lies above Vellandrucia and Tregonning with its distinctive water wheel and is situated near Roseath, Rosemanowes and Gwellandevas Vean, all three having been associated with the Trevales Estates many years ago. Close by is Goonvean – 'the little downland' – known in 1336 as Goenbyghan and in 1607 as Goenveghan. 'The open downland', Goonorman, is a site of ring barrows of great antiquity.

The fields of Trevales are fertile and sheltered; there are numerous springs and a particular delight in any season is the woodland of sunlight and shadows, revealing flora and fauna in abundance. The fringe of the central village is just visible from this sylvan setting and there are extensive views of the surrounding countryside.

References to the settlement suggest that it originally bore the description of Tre-vanathel-os or 'the farm (or homestead) in the broomy spot'. There are variations of this; Trefathlos in 1303, Trefadlos in 1351 and, in the Court Rolls of 1356, Trevatheles or Trevathelos. Towards the latter part of the 14th century the name was appearing as Trefalthis. A Deed of 1351 exists in which:

John de Penhal grants to John de Tresamwell (i.e. Tresamble) all his lands and half acre Cornish in Goenbyghan and Trefadlos to hold to him and his heirs of his body for ever, at a rent of 15d.

The Cornwall Muster Roll of 1569 is a useful source of information and mentions locations in Stithians which are recognisable, albeit with spelling differences, including 'Ressey, 'Ounevean', 'Rosemenewas' and 'Tregonyn'. Unfortunately, Trevales does not feature in the muster certificate under 'Stythens Parryshe within the Hundred of Kerrier' and the likely explanation is that the detail for Trevales was lost due to mutilation or illegibility. Certainly this is a sad loss since the record relates to the reign of Queen Elizabeth I when musters were required of men from each county at the time of the threat of invasion by Spain; the lists provided for the declaration of men in the parishes between the ages of 16 years and '60 score yeres' and required details of horses of specified breeds. However, we do know that there was no parkland or enclosure in the parish at that time for, as one clause states: 'Touching the Acts and Statuts... we have none such within the compas of oure paryshe'.

The Trevales estates were absorbed into the Manor of Penryn Corffe between 1649 and 1758 when the settlement appears variously as Trevallis, Trevalley, Trevialles and eventually Trevales.

Peter Gill held 'Trevallis in Lese' in 1660 when he was taxed at the lowest limit of two shillings on £5 yearly income from land, leases, money and stock. John Gill was assessed with one hearth in 1664 paying two shillings for the year following inspection of his household by the parish constable and the collector. The tax came about because of the shortfall in the king's revenue (although the poor were exempt if they did not pay Church or poor rates and in cases where property or lands were of low value).

In his will of February 1693 (a deposition of 1694 exists), 'Robart Bisshop, husband of Rachell' gave his status as a yeoman and there is reference to his tenements at Trevales, Resigh (Roseath) and Trewithen. He left £3 to be given to the 'poore of the Parish'. Trevales appears also in the will of yeoman John Bishop in September 1715, which records that his tenements of 'Reseath and Reseathvean, Rosemanowes, Trewithan and Trevales' were valued at £120. His inventory tells us something of his way of life: 'a yoak oxen, sixteen cows, seventeen young cattle, fower horses and seven coults, eighteen sheep, corne and haye in the mowhay', plus three-eighths of a share in a

Trevales, 1990s.

Trevales from a postcard, c.1910.

tinwork called Good Speed, bringing the estate's value to £208. At the time of John Bishop's tenancy the farm comprised 41 acres and the land was named Great Field, North Meadow, Great Hill Meadow, Foxes Close, Higher Field, Middle Field, Cross Field, Reed's, Park Rase, Bishop's, Gill's and Little Meadow. The fields were all of arable quality with a very small area of furze.

The law court of the Right Honourable Charles Beville, Earl of Radnor (held for the Manor of Penryn Corffe) recorded, on 4 April 1721:

They present the death of John Bishop, being a life on Trevallis in Stithyans and that therewith a herriott due on his death. They present the houses and hedges on Trevallis to be out of repair and that the tenants have promised to repair the same against the next Court.

From this point on, the estate was passed to his brother, Henry Bishop, whose family subsequently lived at Rosemanowes.

Stephen Andrew, son of William and Ann Andrew, was a tinner of Trevales who appeared in a list of members of the Methodist Society in 1767. The inventory of yeoman John Trelease (1681-1741), a co-tenant of Travales with Walter Reed, valued Trevales at £110 and 'Trewithan house and medow' at £15.

Richard and Jane Reed were the tenants of the 22-acre farm at Nanpean Wartha and their family of three daughters and six sons included Walter Reed who married Margaret Gill of Trevales in 1721; she was the daughter of Nicholas and Welmet Gill. Walter Reed entered into a co-tenancy at Trevales with John Trelease but this arrangement appears to have ceased by 1739 when the names of Walter Reed and Edward Gill (Margaret Gill Reed's uncle) are detailed. Over the years Walter secured a 99-year lease on the major share of Nanpean Wartha from the Bassett family of Tehidy; he purchased Ennis and Carbis and entered into numerous mining ventures as well as being an adventurer in Carnkye Mine. Articles of Agreement in 1743 provided for 32 parts of which Walter Reed held nine and Francis Bassett six, with nine other participants taking the balance.

Wheal Providence in Mullion was another venture where, with others, he secured a sett to search for copper at Predannack Wartha. He also owned the Perran tin-smelting house and in 1760 Captain Walter Reed was advising Mr Bassett of Tehidy Manor on the re-conditioning of Penventon Adit where work continued for some years. The family's involvement in mining continued through Walter's sons. The family was described as:

... having been long what it termed good livers in the Parish who advanced themselves by successful adventures in mines and by conducting a smelting house in the Parish of Perran Arworthall.

Thomas Reed (1735-1812) was the second son of Walter Reed and his involvement in mining included that of leaseholder in Rubby (Wheal Ruby) and Wheal Vernon, Porkellis Bal, as a bounder (holder in tin-bound shares). He secured a lease at Wheal Prosper on Polladras Downs, Breage, and the enterprise opened as Wheal Upton; he is also recorded in deals at the stamping mills of Trenear and Garlidna. Trevales House, a property of great charm and character set in beautiful grounds, was built by Thomas Reed in the 1770s (with later additions). Reed was also responsible for establishing the gardens and plantation. Thomas Reed took out arms in 1787 (*overleaf*) which are featured in the window east of

the south aisle of the church:

> ARMS: VERT, THREE BUNDLES OF REEDS OR, ON A CHIEF ARGENT, TWO CHOUGHS PROPER:
> CREST: ON A MOUNT VERT A GREYHOUND SABLE FROM THE NECK PENDANT A BUGLE HORN STRINGED GOLD.

Thomas Reed drew up his will on 17 October 1807 followed by a codicil on 10 February 1808, witnessed by James Polkinhorn, William Dunstan and William Hellings. However, he was not content and a further codicil was arranged on 18 March 1808 with the witnesses on this occasion being William Dunstan, William Hellings and Thomas Peters. Thomas Reed's signature remains confident and clear and there were no more changes until a codicil on 8 June 1812 when he was near death (as revealed by the sadly altered hand). The vicar of Stithians, Edward Nankivell, his niece, Mary Nankivell James, and James Martin (publican of Stithians) were at hand as witnesses.

On the day of his death Thomas Reed directed yet another change and the last codicil was written down and witnessed on 9 June 1812 when the vicar and his niece were in attendance again, together with William Spargo, publican of Mabe. The document records 'the within testator died about half past 11 o'clock on the night of Tuesday the ninth day of June 1812. Thomas Hocker, nephew and heir of Thomas Reed, took up residence at Trevales House and the 82-acre farm was advertised for let in 1837 (*right*).

In the summer of 1995 Mr and Mrs D. Hillyer, owners of Trevales, were approached by a film company from Germany with a view to using Trevales as a location for the filming of one of the Rosamund Pilcher books. The film, *Voices of Summer*, was intended for audiences in Germany where the Cornish countryside is greatly appreciated. The house was overwhelmed with the paraphernalia of lighting, sound and filming, set building, catering and the make-up and wardrobe departments. A well-known parishioner, Jack Penrose, came into his own and was nominated 'Film Star of Stithians', participating most competently in the film four times – once being filmed from a helicopter!

FRIDAY, MAY 26, 1837

PARISH OF STYTHIANS.

DESIRABLE FARM TO BE LET.

TO BE LET BY SEALED TENDER, for the Term of Fourteen Years from Christmas next, that desirable FARM, called

TREVALES,

In the Parish of Stythians,

Consisting of a good Farm-House, Stable, Cow-Houses, &c., and 82A. 0R. 1P. of good Arable, Meadow, and Pasture Land, statute measure, and now in the occupation of Mr. Joseph Thomas.

The above Estate has the peculiar advantage of being well situated in the centre of the following Market Towns, viz:—Three miles from Penryn, five from Redruth, four from St. Day, five from Falmouth, six from Chacewater, eight from Helston, and nine from Truro; which places are considered to afford the best Markets in the county for the disposal of agricultural produce.

For viewing the Property, apply to the Tenant, and for further information to the Proprietor,

Thomas Hocker,
At Trevales.

TENDERS will be received at Trevales until the 24th day of June next, when the person whose offer is accepted, will be apprized thereof.

N.B.—The Public are requested to take Notice that no verbal offer will be accepted; nor will any promise of the Estate be given to any person previous to the day fixed for opening the respective Tenders.

Trevales, 23rd May, 1837.

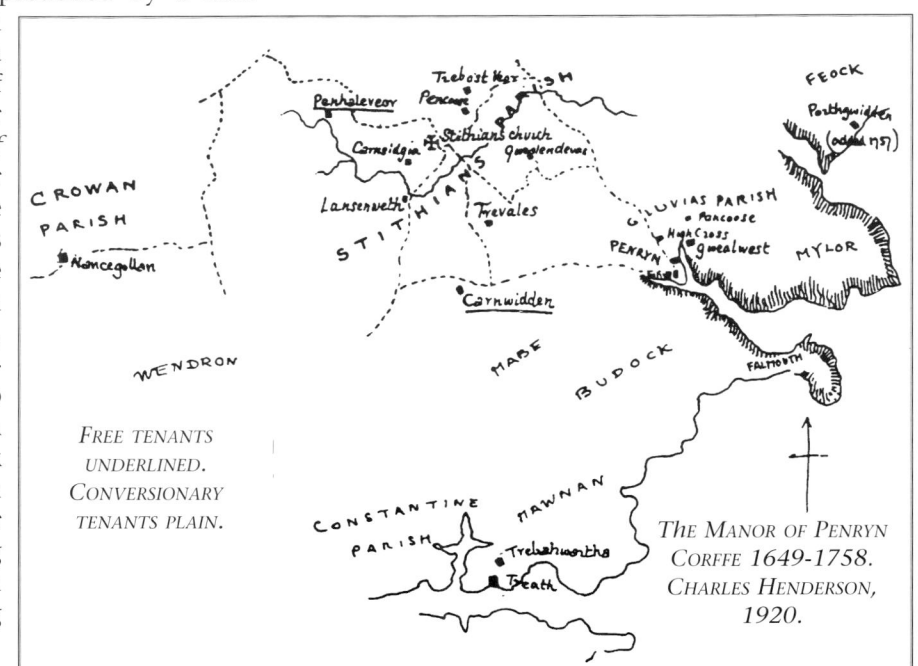

FREE TENANTS UNDERLINED. CONVERSIONARY TENANTS PLAIN.

THE MANOR OF PENRYN CORFFE 1649-1758. CHARLES HENDERSON, 1920.

Chapter 3: Transport

At the turn of the century, there were two waggonettes that carried the villagers of Stithians to Redruth, their nearest town, on Tuesdays and Fridays. One was owned by Mr Sara, of Ennis and Carbis Farm and driven by Mr Kneebone, and the other belonged to Mr Peters of Tremenhere Farm. Sydney Bowden tells us of this in *Book Four, Aspects of the History of Stithians*. When milk factories started to take milk from the farmers to process into butter, the driver started looking for another job as the milk had to be collected so early in the morning!

Led by Mr Jacker Martin of Carn Farm, the farmers bought a redundant horse-drawn Jersey car and secured the top half on the bed of the lorry. They could then take 25 passengers, all in open seats, to the nearest town. This car was named Progress and proved a profitable venture. It was followed by a shining blue 35-seater charabanc called Bluebell. This aroused the interest of four local businessmen, Mr Edgar Polkinhorn (Kennall Flour Mills), Mr J.A. Richards (Kennall Granite Works), Mr Ben Simmons (a butcher from Crellow House) and Mr T.B. Porter of Goonlaze. They bought four large red charabancs, a Leyland motor lorry and a steam-driven vertical boiler truck capable of drawing 20 tons. A large garage was built in the grounds of Crellow and another at Bennets Corner, between the village and Goonlaze, for the lorries. Thus the Red Car Motor Co. was formed, which Mr Simmons and his brother-in-law, Mr Porter, ran for two decades until it was taken over by Western National in 1935.

Two drivers with a friend, seated in the back of the bus. If it rained the hood could be raised from the back over the seats and there was a separate door for each row.

A taxi driven by Mr Porter with Mr Joseph Williams in the front seat and Mr and Mrs Jim Gluyas and Mrs Annie Moyle in the back seat.

Another outing leaving Church Corner at an early date, before the War Memorial was put there. Mr Johnnie Peters was driving the carriage.

TRANSPORT

The Red Car Motor Company

Telegraphic Address—
"Redcars, Stithians."

Above: *One of the choir outings in the new 'Red Car'. Harold Knuckey was the driver.*

Right: *Mr Clifford Wills at the wheel awaiting the return of the trippers.*

Below: *An invoice for the delivery of 12 tons of sand from the lorry.*

Above: *The company's garage at Bennets Corner. Later, Stewart Andrew used it as a granite-cutting shed and then it was used to store farm implements. One moonlit night a motorcyclist mistook the doors for the road and drove right through them and out the other side, missing the machinery and surviving with only minor injuries.*

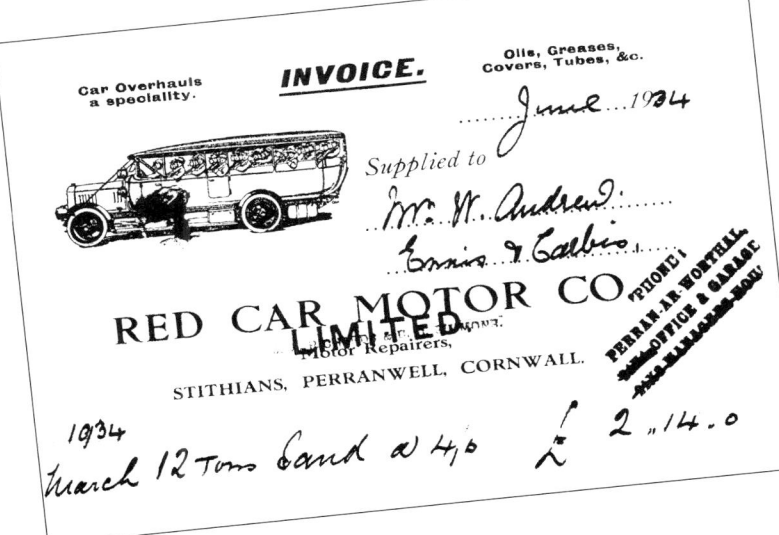

Stithians Parish Church, 1939, and (inset) *the magnificent granite tower from the west, an angle not often portrayed*

A church tea-treat procession with Revd Reginald Frederick Moody at the head. On his left is Mr Joseph Williams followed by a British Army band. This was in 1914, and at the beginning of the First World War, when most of the young men of the parish would have been away in HM armed forces. The photograph was taken on the approach road to the church, and the school and the Seven Stars Hotel can just be made out in the background.

Chapter 4: St Stythians Parish Church

For a village the size of Stithians, albeit having grown considerably over the years, the Parish Church is quite a spacious and roomy one, with a fine granite tower – as fine as any in Cornwall. Built of granite ashlar, or square blocks, it overlooks the ancient village. The north side and nave were built during the first half of the 14th century and the south side and tower in the 15th. This is clearly discernible in the outer fabric of the church as revealed by the different types of granite used in the building processes over the years. It is perhaps the oldest, and was certainly then the largest, edifice in the parish.

Today the church comprises a chancel, nave, north and south aisles and a tower. The tower was built in the early 1400s and has an interior, winding granite staircase leading to the bell chamber.

At the west side of the south entrance to the church is the baptistery where there is an octagonal, 15th-century, granite baptismal font. In 1862 there was a restoration of the chancel. The east window depicts Our Lord's Ascension and is dedicated to Dr William Charles Watson who died in 1898. A large marble plaque on the north wall commemorates William James Benjamin Trewin of Stithians and New Zealand, a barrister and Mayor of Fielding from 1906 to 1910. He died in New Zealand in 1912 and was a relative of the benefactor who bequeathed a large sum of money to St Stythians, enough to finance the inclusion of a four-faced striking clock in the tower and a peal of six bells.

On the north side of the chancel there is another tablet – erected in memory of the Revd William Ralph Daine, MA, vicar of Stithians from 1896 to 1911, and erected by friends to commemorate his ministry. His tragic death, in November 1911, left the parish in a deep state of shock (*see page 26*). Yet another plaque commemorates James Martin who died in 1821, and also his son, the

Revd Francis Arbruthnot Wright, vicar of St Stythians from 1847 to 1877.

Originally there were four bells. However, in 1950 a peal of six bells was dedicated by the Bishop of Truro. The tenor bell was installed in 1790 and the treble and second and third bells in 1930 after being re-cast by Messrs Taylor of Loughborough. The fourth and fifth bells were installed in 1950.

The Church Features

Clockwise from above: *The fine organ; An Elizabethan chalice (part of St Stythians' plate); the memorial on the north side of the chancel, in memory of William Ralph Daine, MA, TCD; the beautiful east window and high altar; the small stone building in the west end of the churchyard, in the north wall of which was a small 13th-century window with some carved stonework. Possibly it has been rebuilt at some stage, or may even be the remnants of a priest's house; the Lady Chapel, also known as the 'Cumber Memorial Chapel', erected by William G. Cumber in memory of his sister, Daisy Emma Deverell; marble monument on the north wall in memory of William James Benjamin Trewin; the baptismal font. The fine oak cover is in memory of Helen Hellings, who died in 1928 – a much-loved Sunday-School teacher as well as a teacher at the day school where her sister, Jane (Janie), was head of the Infants' and Girls' School at that time. Helen's untimely death left a grieving parish in its wake.*

Honourable James Martin, known as the 'Father of Gawler', Southern Australia. Gawler has only recently become 'twinned' with Stithians in honour of James Martin's memory.

The oak font cover was placed in the church in memory of Helen Hellings who, as organist and Sunday-School teacher, as well as Secretary of the Church Council, served her church devotedly until her death in 1928. She was also a teacher in the Day School.

The contents of an old inventory of church 'goods' at St Stythians, in the third year of the reign of Edward VI (1547-53), reveals:

Church Possessions in the 16th Century Church Goods: Stediance

This is the trew Inventorie of the goodes of the Churche of Stedyance from the 15th day of February unto the 22nd day of April, anno tertia Dom Edwardi sexti, Dei Gratia Anglie, Thrace et Hiberni Regis, Fidii Defensoor et in terra ratio Anglicanumi et Hiberni sub capite.
In Premis: 3 bells
Item: ii chalices of silver
ii pere of Vestments of Whyte Damaske
one cope of blue Velvet [the usual colour of copes of that period, just before and after the Reformation].
one pere brasse chanters
two serples
three towels
one pere of crewetts of tynn
one senser of Laten
one crymetery of Lede (the lead basin in the font, still to be found in the church).
one stremer of Redde sylke

John Reskymer, John Godolphin, John Killigrew.

Stediance, or Stedyance, was the old pronunciation of Stithians, or Stythians. There are many variations and some older folk may still know them.

The year 1950 saw the restoration of the tower and its subsequent dedication by the Bishop of Truro. At the same time the peal of six bells and the four-faced clock were restored, the Lady Chapel consecrated and the organ repaired. This instrument was a re-conditioned, one-manual, electrically-blown organ.

In July 1980 the very fine organ from the closed Hendra Wesleyan Chapel was offered to the Parochial Church Council and was installed in October 1981. The organ is a memorial to the late Canon Jack Jose, vicar of Stithians from 1955 to 1979. With the organ came the free-standing marble Collins Memorial, and these two are now in the south aisle.

The Vicarage

Rebuilt in 1771, the previous house had been a thatched and stone-walled house. There were four ground-floor rooms, earth floored, with three rooms and a half-chamber above the main hall. The glebe land totalled $37\frac{1}{2}$ acres plus two gardens and two mowhays. The rebuilt Vicarage has since been sold by the Church Commissioners after which it became a carvery.

During this period the incumbent resided in the Vicarage at Perran-ar-Worthal, the daughter church to that at Stithians. Gwennap Parish Church has since been included with those of Stithians and Perran-ar-Worthal and a new Vicarage built close to, and almost opposite, St Stythians.

Parish Church Choir, c.1970. Left to right, back: Miss Ruby Martin (organist), Ian Tremayne, Joy Penaluna, Felicity Prowse, Revd Jack Jose, Bridget Prowse, David Phillips, Stephen Tremayne, Mr S. Percival (choirmaster); front: Nigel Dunstan, Symon Dunstan, Belinda Ivey, Joanna Biscoe, Lynne Dunstan, Jane Acton, Lesley Pascoe, ?, Philip Pascoe.

Tragedy in Stithians

Below: *Reverend William Ralph Daine, MA, and his American-born wife, Mary Meacham Daine, both of whom have memorials in the church. Revd Daine made possible the building of the Sunday schools at Stithians and Perran-ar-Worthal and was vicar of St Stythians from 1896 to 1911, when he was tragically killed in an accident while attempting to pull up the runaway horses of a horse-drawn omnibus in which both he and his wife were passengers. The accident occurred on the descent of Buller Hill on the Stithians to Redruth road on 24 November, when the horses, frightened by a steamroller working on the road, bolted. Revd Daine was thrown at a bend in the road and killed instantly – he is buried in the churchyard. However, his wife survived and died in 1915 in Syracuse, New York, USA, after serving faithfully in Stithians for many years.*

Bottom: *the omnibus from which Reverend Daine was thrown, seen here after the accident outside a wheelwright's shop in Redruth (pictures from the* Daily Sketch *newspaper, 27 November 1911).*

Above: *Church choir outing to Bude and Clovelly c.1936 with the Reverend William Fenwick Ord Kirk (in trilby hat and raincoat). Revd Kirk was vicar of Stithians from 1934-44. His elder son, Ian, is on his left.*

CORNISH VICAR KILLED IN HEROIC ATTEMPT TO SAVE HIS WIFE IN RUNAWAY OMNIBUS ACCIDENT.

Church tea treat, 1916, with teas laid out on the lawns in front of the Vicarage. The small child in front is Kathleen Holman – with her mother, Mrs Elizabeth (Bessie) Holman, seated behind her. In the picture are three generations of one family, Mrs Harriet Mary Corey and her mother, Mrs Jane Williams, and daughter, Winifred Jane, all of Carncrees Farm. Also in the picture are: Emmie Peters, Mrs Janie Peters, Mrs E. Andrew, Mrs H. Andrew, Mrs M. Reynolds, Mr C. Holman, Miss Nora Way and Mrs Martin of Carnsiddia Farm, whose husband, Mr Henry Martin, was a churchwarden for many years.

A nativity play presented by the Girls' Friendly Society, 1946. The producer was Mrs E.M. Phillips. Left to right, back: Peggy Phillips, Betty Gilkes, Marlene Eddy, Mary Stapleton, Mrs E.M. Phillips, Olive Stribley, Christine Andrew, Ann Andrew, Margaret Phillips, Alison Corey; middle: Jean Bowden, Pamela Thomas, Shirley Thomas, Kathleen Clemens, Gwladys James, Elizabeth (Lee) Prowse, Gloria Stapleton, Dawn Thomas; front: Ann Thompson, Mary Clemens, Vivienne Noye, Lucille Combellack, Velia Brooks, Heather Pascoe, Barbara Bray, Joycelyn Dunstan.

The Sunday School resting at Tretheague after walking behind the bands from chapel, c.1895 (photo RCI). Accounts at that time show that they would order 70 dozen tea-treat buns and 650 16-oz. cakes to be baked by Mr George. There would be five visitors' tables and four for the teachers, and tea would be 9d. for visitors and 6d. for others. This was held in a field at Carn Farm owned by Mr J. Martin where a bandstand was made from two wagons. Afterwards there would be sports and games for the children.

Representatives of the chapels in the Gwennap circuit at a quarterly meeting at Carharrack Methodist Chapel in the 1920s. Stithians people include: Mesdames W.J. Martin and J. Richards and Messrs T. Opie, W.J. Martin, S. Oliver, J. Collins, E.C. Dunstan and J.C. Paddy Ponsanooth.

Chapter 5: Methodism

John Wesley first visited Stithians in 1744 when the influence of the Parish Church was at an all-time low. The Bishop's visitation returns for the church in that year states that there were 140 families in Stithians and no dissenters, there were 120 communicants and one service each Sunday with a sermon every fortnight alternating with Perran-ar-Worthal, where the curate lived. The vicar, Revd Thomas Hearle, MA, lived at St Michael Penkivel so he had to cross the river Fal to make his rare visits to his parish. There were no public schools but the children were catechised on Sunday afternoons in the summer season. John Wesley states in his journal that he visited Stithians five times between 1744 and 1750, always preaching to the people, and if it was on a Sunday, he would attend a service in the church. Once he had to hide behind a hedge because a mob from Gwennap were after him and on another occasion, while he was still preaching, the constables and the churchwardens came and pressed one of the hearers into service. Charles Wesley twice visited Stithians in 1746 and by 1767, 30 members of the society had petitioned the Methodist Conference for help. By 1774 there was a quarterly payment from 40 members for the sum of 15s.6d. by the steward, John Jenkins. Miles, in his *Chronological History of Methodism* (Fourth edition, 1814), tells us that there was a chapel in existence in 1786. It has been thought that there was a thatched building on the site of the schoolroom at Hendra. There was a Bishop's licence for a house at Stithians in 1808, and a further licence for a newly-erected house was given on 14 March 1815 – this was, of course, the main chapel at Hendra.

The new chapel was built at a time of a great revival of Methodism throughout the west of Cornwall. The Revd William Booth states in a letter to a friend:

> ... in the early part of the year 1799, a powerful awakening commenced in the western part of the county, extending almost immediately to Redruth, and continuing for the next six months. As a result of which the Methodist societies in the Redruth circuit, which then embraced Falmouth, Truro and Camborne, added to their numbers 2350 persons, increasing from 2500 to 4850 members. A still more glorious effusion of the Holy Spirit took place in the spring of the year 1814.

Mr Joseph Martin of Tretheague gave the land for the chapel and the cemetery and was a class leader and a trustee. Hendra Chapel was enlarged in c.1844 and in 1864 the walls raised and a new roof put on. Over the next 50 years Methodism developed all over Cornwall – by 1834 there were 13 circuits, 25 ministers, 18 122 members of society and about 1900 children in the Sunday schools, 290 local preachers, 220 chapels and an estimated 55 000 hearers.

In 1991 the President of the Methodist Conference visited Stithians Methodist Church for celebrations of 125 years in the parish. Left to right: Revd Colin Allen, David Green, Revd Donald English (President), Tony Langford, Colin Roberts, Paul Gluyas.

By 1851 Stithians was on the Gwennap plan with services at 9.30am and 6pm on Sundays and with a meeting on Wednesdays at 7pm. Foundry was a small meeting house in the village with a service at 2.30pm, and Gear, a small hamlet on the road to Gwennap, had a chapel run by local farmers with services at 2.30pm and 6pm on Sundays and on Thursdays at 7pm. In 1863 an unfortunate division took place in the Stithians Wesleyan Society between people of different opinions about the Sunday School tea treat (and involving part of a movement within the area of a more democratic branch of Methodism).

This is recorded in a booklet written at the time by Mr Nicholas Odgers, and it was the beginning of the United Methodist Free Church in Stithians. They joined the Redruth Fore Street circuit with their own ministers and local preachers and built a new chapel across the road. A three-storey building holding 800 people and costing £1200, it was opened on 26 September 1866. These two chapels served the inhabitants of the parish with small chapels also running at Gear and Gribbas, Penhalvean (on the Gwennap plan) and Foundry (in the care of Penmennor).

Hendra Chapel

Above: *Hendra Wesleyan Chapel built in 1815.*

Above right: *Children and teachers outside Hendra Chapel for a Sunday-School treat, 1910.*

Right: *Interior of Hendra Chapel before the door to the Sunday School was added.*

Below: *A group at Hendra Sunday-School treat, with Mr Thomas Opie Supt. on the extreme right (half kneeling).*

METHODISM

Top: *Drama at Hendra in 1940. Left to right, standing: O. Knuckey, I. Dunstan, B. Brown, L. Dunstan, G. Hall, A. Bennets, L. Ford, B. Knuckey; seated: S.N. Richards, E. Perry, J. Stephens, W.J. Martin, Pastor and Mrs Martland, J. Perry, N. Ford, J. Dunstan; front: R. Brown, L. Ford, R. Stephens.*

Above: *In 1964 Hendra Chapel celebrated their 150th Anniversary with a thanksgiving service and tea when a cake was cut by the two oldest members – Mrs John Richards and Mrs Mabel Peters (with the Revd Ian Haile looking on).*

Above: *In 1976, after the Redevelopment Commission asked for a reduction in the number of churches in the Redruth Circuit, the Ministries Sub-Committee hoped that Stithians would have a single Methodist church. After much discussion and prayer, Hendra Church Council decided to discontinue services at the end of March. This photograph was taken after the closing service with the Revd S. Underhill, Mrs B. Knuckey, Mrs C. Veall, Mrs L. Ford, Mr A. Ford and Mr O. Knuckey.*

United Methodist Free Church

Left: *Mr William Henry Gluyas, 1931. He had been a trustee of the Stithians United Methodist Free Church since 1877 and in 1902 his wife became the Chapel Keeper with a salary of £9 per year. They moved into the new cottage which the church had decided to build in the north corner of the moor in 1878. Tenders were accepted from F. Vincent and J. Collins (masons) for £56.5s.0d. and from Peters (carpenter) for £358.8s.0d. John Bath was offered £2 for enough stone to build the house.*

William Henry was self taught and very well read. He always sat in the leader's seat in the front of the chapel and when he prayed he would lose his stammer, which was very noticeable at all other times. He held every office in the chapel and Sunday School and on his 80th birthday the young ladies of his bible class presented him with an armchair.

Right: *Mr John Gluyas, son of William Henry. John looked after his father after his mother died and was caretaker of the chapel for 37 years. He was not a strong man but the chapel was his life. He was also a postman and he walked many miles each day for 12 shillings a week. During the First World War he wrote a letter each month to every young man from the parish who was in the forces and he often added a little money for a packet of Woodbines.*

He spent hours training the Sunday School children to recite and sing for the anniversary of the chapel and he also helped in the Sunday School. This was held in the afternoon and if any child was late they would lose their mark for that day. There was also a task hearer's book and each child had to recite so many verses of a hymn or scripture – at the end of the year the ones who had gained the highest number of marks would get the best prize, a 2s.6d. book.

METHODISM

Above: *UMFC choir on the steps of the chapel (right), c.1901. Left to right, back: W.T. Spargo, W. Odgers, S. Bailey, P. Pascoe, J. Sarah; 3rd row: F. Sincock, W. Opie, J.H. Bowden, F. and J. Trerise, L. Knuckey; 2nd row: J. Dunstan, M. Spargo, M. Knuckey, L. Williams, M. Bath, M.J. Opie, M.H. Gluyas; front: B. Dunstan, R. Trerise, L. Peters, L.H. Pascoe.*

Above: *Two miners on their donkey shay outside the UMFC with the caretaker's house in the background. Mr W.H. Gluyas made and repaired boots and shoes in the little shop there (from a postcard by Govier from the RIC, early 1900s).*

Left: *Leaders of the UMFC in the 1920s. Left to right, back: Francis Gluyas, Richard Andrew, William Henry Gluyas; front: John Reed, Revd Urwin, Henry Choak, William T. Opie.*

Penmennor

Left: *The Memorial Hall built onto the chapel in 1929 at a cost of £695.7s.0d. There was a new cloakroom upstairs and a boiler room for the central heating as well as an open garage below. A tablet inside gave the names of the men who fell in the First World War.*

Right: *Cast of one of the religious plays produced at Penmennor during the 1950s. Left to right, back: L. Combellack, M. Eddy, V. Bowden, B. Gluyas, M. Waters; standing: R. Pascoe, H. Dunstan, H. Pascoe, F. Bolitho, B. Pearse, W. Gluyas, M. Pascoe, R. Mitchell, T. Wills, Pastor J. Mitchell, K. Andrew; seated: M. Bath, K. Pascoe, G. Spargo, J. Gluyas, M. May, M. Dunstan, J. Williams, R. Bowden, M. Bolitho, K.M. Bowden, E. May.*

Left: *Penmennor Chapel Choir in the 1940s. They sang Handel's Messiah in the chapel with every seat filled and they sang at many musical festivals around the county winning 12 first- and 3 second-place prizes in 15 competitions.*

Right: *A choir trip to Lands End in 1926 in a 'Red' bus which ran a service from the company's depot in Stithians.*

Chapel Outings

Left: *A tea-treat procession in 1908 on the way to Carn Farm where there were low forms for the children to sit on to eat their buns. They were served tea or lemonade from earthenware pitchers. Note the entrance gate to the Sunday School and Mr Odger's pigsty, now all removed.*

Right: *A tea treat in 1938. Left to right: Nick Pascoe, Lewis Pascoe, James Andrew, Bill Andrew, Anne Walker, Mary Andrew, Hilda Andrew, Margaret Kirk, Percy Andrew, Joyce Andrew, Ethel Andrew, little Ronnie Pascoe (in front). In the background is Mr Ripper's ice-cream cart.*

Left: *A group of leaders at a treat, c.1915. Left to right, standing: Mr Oliver, Mrs J.D. Pascoe, Mr Jim Gluyas, Mrs R. Reed, Mr R. Andrew, Mrs J. Andrew, Mr S. Oliver; seated: Mrs Oliver, Mrs E. Harper, ?, Mrs E. Andrew, Mrs S. Oliver.*

Right: *An early chapel outing from the Churchtown. The horse bus is being driven by its owner, Mr Henry Sara (of Ennis and Carbis Farm), who kept the vehicle at Tretheague.*

Mr Horace Dunstan delivering milk to the houses in the village.

Milk suppliers and staff at the Golden Lion Cheese Factory, late 1920s. This was a new venture organised by the farmers to take their milk. Later the Milk Marketing Board built a factory at Camborne and made butter there. Left to right, back: W. Chittock of Penhalurick, C. Williams of Trewince, B. Corey of Carncrees, H. Oliver of Colvennor, C. Tozer of Tretheague, W. Opie of Lansenwith, J. Winn of Tregolls, B. Thomas of Menerdue;
centre: Sam Williams of Trewince, Dale Tremough, Lawrey Penhalveor, L. Oliver of Crosspost Farm, W. Tresidder of Menerdue, J. Jones of Menerdue;
front: Miss Nankervis of Lancarrow Hill, J. Oliver of Penmennor, Miss A. Downing of Penhalvean, E. Toy of Lansenwith, J. Knuckey of Penhalveor, H. Choak of Trelusback, Miss Oliver, D. Ivey of Menherion, Grace Nankivel of Lancarrow.

Chapter 6: Agriculture

Stithians is an unspoilt Cornish village untouched by through roads. The scenery has changed little over the past 400 years and is dominated by green fields and lovely Cornish hedges built with waste granite stones from the quarries. The parish covers 4361 acres (including the reservoir), nearly all of which is cultivated (due to the high number of smallholdings which have grown up here over the years). Often such holdings came about for the simple reason that there were no working mines within the parish and so the miners had to have a pony or donkey to take them to work. In turn, they needed some grazing land and they would invariably have a few hens and a pig to eat up the scraps. Gradually a little more land would be broken in and they would get a cow. Then, at a later date, they would rent some cows from a local farmer and so slowly climb the farming ladder. Over the centuries the ownership of the land has changed greatly and the manorial history of Stithians is a complicated affair; at least a dozen manors have claimed jurisdiction over parts of the parish at various times – some farms were even divided between manors. However, four major manors can be identified: Arworthal, Kennall, Penryn Corffe and Tretheague. These estates have been sold off over the years and the smaller farms have developed. In 1866 there were 1115 cattle in the parish of Stithians, 628 sheep, 540 pigs and an unknown number of poultry. By 1936, there were 2209 cattle, 51 sheep, 3334 pigs and 18 987 head of poultry. This was during an era when small mixed farms were thriving but all has now changed. Land fertility has improved and more corn is grown, milk can only be produced up to quota from the European order and all bacon factories in the area have closed down. Poultry farming is only profitable on a large scale and beef has been hit by the BSE crisis, so the days of the small family unit are over and farms of 200-400 acres with modern machinery are the order of the day.

Above: *Corn mows out in the field were built to protect the grain if the weather was too wet to bring it in to the rick.*
Below: *A three-horse whim used to grind corn in the barn at Mount Wise Farm. There were several like this in the area, at Rosemanowes and Ennis and Carbis Farm.*

The village blacksmith at Hendra was working on the left-hand side of the road between the two chapels and beside James Martin's carpenter's shop. John Odger was there in 1856 and his son was there until the 1930s.

Inset: Bringing in the sheaves of corn with a horse and wain at Seaureaugh Farm and (main picture) threshing the corn at Rosemanowes Farm after it had been brought in to a rick in the mowhay. This task would take about 15 men, all needing to be fed by the farmer's wife afterwards.

AGRICULTURE

 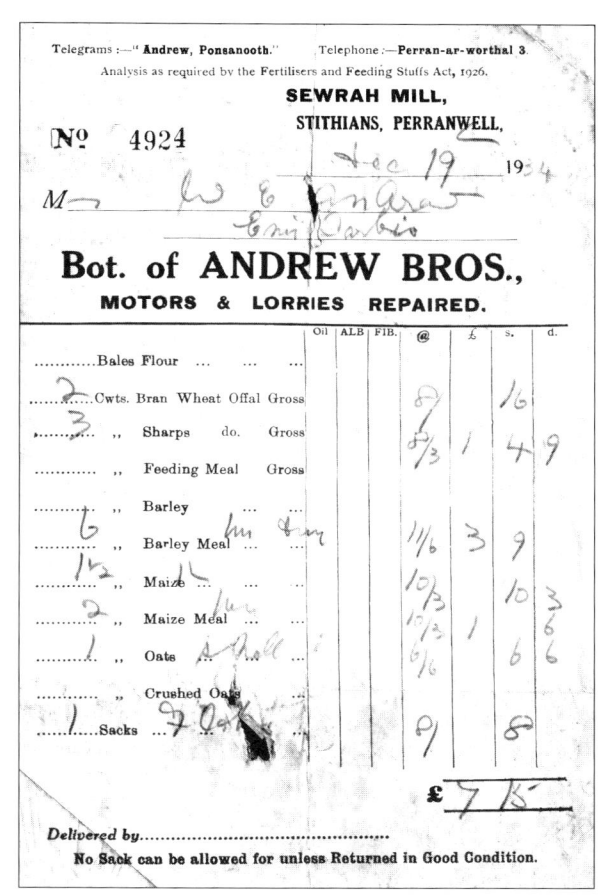

Above: *The water wheel at Sewrah (or Ripper's) mill which was used to grind the corn for the local farmers (by kind permission of the RIC) and (right) bill from Andrew Bros of Sewrah Mill, 1932.*

Ennis and Carbis Farm, c.1900, with the stable mounting block (or hepping stock) at one end and the Seven Stars pub at the other (built by the farmer in the early 1800s). The farm covers 34 acres and in the 1920s and '30s villagers bought their milk and cream there from Mr and Mrs William Andrew.

Above: *Feeding chickens hatched out in the coops at Seaureaugh Farm in 1929. This was before day-old chicks could be bought.*

Left: *Typical work for the farmer's wife in the 1920s and '30s – washing all the parts of the separator which was used to separate the cream from the fresh milk (which was then scalded in a pan on a steamer on the Cornish range and put in the dairy to cool). The next day it was churned by hand to make butter. The buttermilk was drawn off and washed several times to get the milk out, then rolled on a wooden worker, weighed and made into pats. This was one of the many labour-intensive jobs for the farmer's wife.*

Above: *Going home to milk the cows after helping your neighbour with the threshing. Adjoining farmers helped each other on these busy days.* Inset: *Milking out in the field at Rosemanowes Farm.*

AGRICULTURE

STITHIANS AGRICULTURAL ASSOCIATION

No pictorial history of the parish would be complete without priority being given to Stithians Show. It has been in existence since 1834 and has been held every year without a break, except for the time of the two world wars. The Show is always held on Feast Monday (the Monday following the Sunday closest to 13 July). Relatives of families in the village always hope to be home on or near that date and they often come from different parts of the world.

The earliest press report available is from the *West Briton* of 27 July 1838 when it was stated that:

Stithians Annual Show Fair was held in the Churchtown on Monday 16th instant, when the day being fine, great numbers of respectable farmers and butchers, from the neighbouring parishes and towns, attended and a great many bargains were effected at good prices.

At that time the Show may have been held on the village green, today located at the site of the school and the Village Hall. Within living memory, however, it has always been held at Ennis and Carbis Farm with the entrance through the yard gate to the first two fields. When the Association was first formed, with its annual exhibition, there was also an auction of primestock. In time it became a show only and the cattle were said to be 'of the best quality and breed'. The horses and colts meanwhile 'would have done honour to the First Exhibition in the Kingdom'.

The Show has developed in a remarkable way over the years, many generations of the same families from the farming and non-farming communities having given their time and energy each year to make it one of the largest one-day events of its type in the country – a truly great success story. In 1938 the playing field was used for the first time but later more fields were needed from Ennis and Carbis Farm and the glebe land as more people came to visit and exhibit. More car parks were also needed.

By 1927 there were sections for poultry, horticulture, cattle and horses, and the first female members of the Association were recorded in the minutes of a meeting on 5 February 1934. It was these pioneering ladies who founded the domestic section. In 1959 a cage birds section was formed, followed by a dog section in 1965, a goats section in 1968, Young Farmers in 1981, rabbits in 1988 and, most recently, the sheep section, which was started in 1998 after a very long period without any interest being shown. Trade stands from the farming and commercial industries are also now a big part of the Show.

Sheep being shown in 1921 – this is a class of Devon and Cornwall Longwools (photograph from the RIC).

The secretary's hut in the first field at Ennis and Carbis in 1927, with Mr W.F. Andrew, owner of the farm, and Mr John Martin of Carn Farm outside (photographs from the RIC).

A group photographed in 1934 at the Centenary Show, opened by Lieut Comm. P.G. Agnew, MP. Left to right: W.J.T. Peters, ?, R. Martin, J.S. Richards, B.W. Knuckey, ?, W. Andrew, ?, H. Mitchell, Lieut Comm. Agnew, ?, C.J. Cooke, ?, Revd Kirk, J. Richards, W. Opie, Miss J. Hellings, Mrs W.J. Martin, Miss D. Andrew, Miss B. Henderson, Miss K. Holman.

AGRICULTURE

*Members of the Association at a garden fête in the grounds of Crellow House, 1934.
Left to right, back: W.H. Bowden, Howard Phillips, L.G. Sarah, M. Harvey, T. Penaluna, C. Spargo, C. Dunstan, H. Dunstan, W.T. Bowden, Edgar Phillips, R. Wills, Harold Phillips, Wilfred Prowse, A. Dunstan; 3rd row: J.T. Jelbert, D. Bowden, T. Berryman, R. Trerise, B. Odgers, C. Mead, A. Trevena, J. Pascoe, Miss F. Jelbert, E. Trerise, Miss F. Henderson, R. Phillips, Mrs D. Bowden, Miss D. Andrew, W. Manhire, F. Collins, H. Trerise; 2nd row: J.P.A. Harvey, W. Andrew, W.J.T. Peters, Mrs E. Andrew, Mrs O. Knuckey, W.J. Kneebone, Mrs J.S. Richards, Miss J. Hellings, Mrs H. Mitchell, Miss C. Berriman, Miss R. Martin, Nick Johns, R.C. Reed, L. Pascoe; front: Messrs W. Opie, F. Dunstan, F.F. Perry, C.J. Cook, H. Mitchell, J.S. Richards, B.W. Knuckey, W.J. Opie, ?, J. Richards, Ray Berryman, B. Simmons.*

Stithians Agricultural Association, 1993. Left to right, back: Mrs P.M. Bell, Mrs E.F. Bowden, G.C. Downing, Mrs J. Thomason, C.J. Bell, W.T.G. Tresidder, Mrs H.M. Roskilly, Mrs H. Opie, Mrs M. Hadwin, Mrs N.M. Wilson, Mrs J.A. Cockerham, Mrs K. Caddy, C.P. Caddy, C.P. Odgers, G.C. Ellis; 3rd row: J.T. Jelbert, R.M. Berryman, S. Leam, B. Martin, Mrs E. Jones (JP), B. Dale, N.J. Jeffery, Mrs J. Green, R. Pascoe, H.D.J. Reed, W. Prowse, P.J.R. Stephens, J.R. Knuckey (JP); 2nd row: P. Cockerham, H.E. Phillips, N. Wilson, Mrs K. Tremayne, L.A. Roskilly, Mrs J. Brown, W. Williams, M. Opie, C. Opie, P. Brown, T. Williams, K. Wilcocks, H. Martin, S. Tremayne, E.H. Opie, W. Tremayne; front: H.D. Martin, J.M. Tumbull, J.C. Spargo, Jack R. Williams, T.K. Plummer (Hon. Gen. Sec.), H. Kneebone (Chairman), W.P. Gluyas (President), Mrs J. Gluyas, Miss K. Mead (Hon. Treas.), M. Symonds, L.R. Baxter, J.C.D. Oates, A. Opie, Dr C.A. Biscoe.

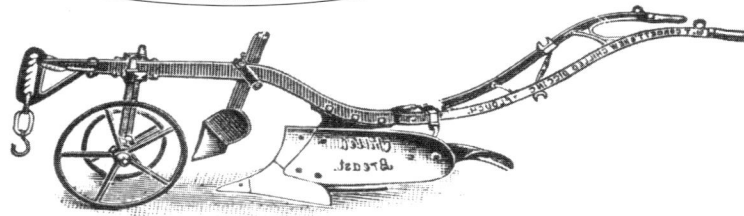

Above: *Typical scene of the show in the 1930s – the grandstand with the flags flying, the cattle being shown in the first field and the cars around the ring or just parked by the hedge (which would have been cheaper). All cars came in through the farm entrance and pedestrians entered through a turnstile which was hired for the first time in 1895 (photo from Camera Craft, Truro).*

Above left: *St Stythians Silver Band at the show in the late 1960s.*

Left: *Gerald Reed, Hon. General Secretary, and A. Opie with the silver cups to be presented to the horse- and cattle-section winners in the late 1950s.*

Chapter 7: School Days

Stithians School began life in 1869 under the watchful eye of master, Louis Martin, as a single-roomed building for boys, girls and infants. In 1870 the government granted financial aid, and required that school logs be kept, the first of which was begun on 2 August 1869. With attendance increasing daily, the first logbook entries make for a healthy picture of the school:

August 2   6 children admitted today.
August 3   4 children admitted today.
August 18   The majority of the children belong to the mining class with a few labourers and stonecutters.
August 19   The attendance is excellent.
August 20   The school just showing the effects of discipline as the children were very rough at first and they are getting a little more orderly.
August 26   Many little children are still coming in for which a gallery would be of some service.
September 6   3 children admitted today. Over 100 children have been admitted since the school opened.
September 13 Number over 130.
September 15 The spelling and dictation require great attention as the children call the hard words anything that is first thought of.
December 10   A school at the Foundry will take away many young children and that with the two schools will considerably reduce mine although I trust it will only be temporarily.

As the final entry here shows, two other schools appeared at this point. One was at Foundry, probably a dame school of some considerable size, and the other at the chapel (possibly the United Methodist Free Church). Plans emerged for a proposed new board school and in 1872 a School Board was formed. The year 1891 saw the Education Act passed which introduced free, compulsory education for all children. Two new classrooms were added to the old school in 1894, and a pair of new cloakrooms during harvest recess.

School Life in the 19th Century

John was five years old. The year was 1898. The day started (as most days did when you were a child then), with mother coming to wake the children and get them downstairs and dressed for school. John lived in a typical Cornish cottage with no running water, no electricity and an outside toilet. He would have had a quick wash of hands and face in an enamel bowl (with water fetched, more than likely, from the village pump). Breakfast was probably a small basin of bread and milk with a sprinkling of pepper and salt, followed by a piece of bread spread with dripping. Then John was off to school for nine o'clock with the sound of the school bell ringing in his ears. Like all of his friends, John walked to school. Some even walked up to and, perhaps, over, three miles in all weathers. School commenced at nine o'clock, there was a playtime at half-past ten until eleven. Lunchtime was at twelve until half-past one and another playtime followed in the middle of the afternoon. John would have gone home at half-past three during his first year in school.

He wrote on a piece of slate about 12 inches by 8 inches encased in a wooden frame and with a pencil also made of slate. He learned his alphabet and his multiplication tables parrot-fashion by chanting them in unison with all his classmates every morning. This constant, daily repetition would have been a very good way of committing lessons to memory.

Top: *Christmas party for the Senior Citizens, c.1966. Servers from the left: Joy Penaluna, Bridget Prowse, Tina Crone. Seated at back from left: Mr Cooke, Mrs W. Peters, Mr Willie Gluyas, Mrs Cooke, Mr W. Peters, Mrs Mary Williams; seated, centre: Mrs Berryman, Mrs G. Williams, Mrs Kelly.*

Above: *Stithians School, 1999.*

Stithians Boys' School, 1896. Left to right, back: Mike Martin, Fred Martin, ?, ?, ?, ? Williams, ? Richards, ? Bath, ? Odgers, W. Peters, ? Sara;
centre: ?, ? Phillips, ? Richards, ? Simmons, ? Alonzo Dunstan, ? Trerise, ? Bath, J.D. Pascoe, ?, Edwin Martin, Edwin Trerise, ?;
front: Mr Kelynack (headmaster), Arthur Martin, ? Martin, Joe Gilbert, Arthur Johns, Willie Opie, ? Knuckey, ? Collins, T. Pascoe, ? Spargo, ? Tozer, ? Eva, ? Odgers, ? Hugh Peters (teacher), Lillian Luke (teacher).

Stithians Girls' School, 1900. Left to right, back: Gertie Opie, Lily Triggs, Lily Reed, Martha Dunstan, Elizabeth Dunstan, Louie Eddy, Janie Dunstan, Maggy Eade, Elsie Richards, Mary Gay, Katie Berryman, Annie Andrew, Tizzie Reed;
centre: Miss J. Jelbart, Winnie Vivian, Winnie Knuckey, Lena Knuckey, Annie Eade, ?, Ellen M. Bath, Fanny Bath, Mary Bath, Cora Pascoe, Emma Pascoe, Nellie Bailey, Millie Allen, Miss Martin;
front: Katie Collins, Mary Collins, Ethel Allen, Sarah Peters, Beatie Dunstan, Ellen Cowling, Lizzie Gluyas, Janie Gluyas, Sarah Reed, Annie Odgers, Laura Mewton, Florrie Collins, Annie Vivian.

SCHOOL DAYS

There was just a play yard outside the school and the girls mostly played with wooden hoops, skipping ropes and bat and ball. Boys played games with marbles, spinning tops and iron hoops. Then there were games like 'tig-in-the-back', hop-scotch, leap frog, etc. The yard was divided by a wall, one side for the girls and one side for the boys.

John and his class mates would have sat at small tables in equally small chairs whilst in the infant class. He progressed up through the school by standards one-six and x-six as well as standard seven, and he remained at school until he was 14 years of age. In standard one, each morning commenced with a scripture lesson in the classroom. There was no assembly or main hall, just the classrooms, the cloakrooms and the toilets which were outside. The children all wore heavy boots, girls as well as boys. When John progressed into standard one he had to stay at school until four o'clock in the afternoon. By this time he would have been using an exercise book and writing with pen and ink. During the winter months the old black, cast-iron combustion stoves were lit to heat the classrooms. These were cylindrical and about three feet in height and often belched smoke and soot into the classrooms. They burned coal and coke.

Reading, writing and arithmetic, with a little history and geography, were daily lessons. Algebra was taught in standard six upwards and maybe a little geometry. Each day, at the end of lessons and just before going home, each class would sing the hymn, 'Now The Day is Over'.

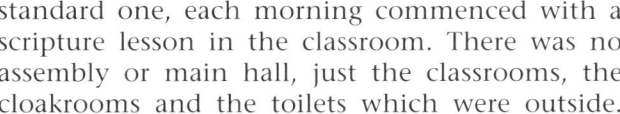

Teachers and pupil teachers, c.1900.
The picture includes: Miss Janie Hellings (back left),
Miss Helen Hellings (back right), Miss M. Allen
(front left) and Miss M. Hicks (front right).

School Life in the 20th Century

In 1902 school boards were replaced with local education authorities (LEAs). In 1917 the Boys' School was amalgamated with the Girls' and Infants' School owing to the fact that the headmaster, Mr Harry Mitchell, had been called away on active service. Miss Janie Hellings then assumed temporary headship.

At one stage (c.1900) the school was able to boast something of an anomaly in having four sets of sisters amongst its teaching staff – the Misses Jane and Helen Hellings, Beatrice and Ethel Peters, Elizabeth and Janie Gluyas and Millie and Lottie Allen. Evacuees from Bermondsey and Walthamstow were absorbed into the school with their teachers during the Second World War and the establishment inevitably became very overcrowded with not a great deal in the way of serious work being achieved. At times, the pupils were even left to their own devices to play games, and school was great fun.

In March c.1950 the school choir broadcast on radio in 'Children's Hour' under their conductor, Mr K. Drayton, and in 1955 a new venture was undertaken by the headmaster, Mr Jack R. Williams. He devised a plan to raise funds by means of a Christmas concert given by the children. The proceeds from the concerts were used to provide the senior citizens of the parish with a Christmas party and a Christmas high tea, as well as a large, decorated Christmas tree laden with gifts, one for each senior citizen present. The children entertained the older folk and waited at table. This proved to be a huge success and was, for the next 19 years, a highlight of the youngsters' school life. Sadly, however, upon the retirement of Mr Williams as headmaster, the festivities were no longer provided. Major alterations and improvements were carried out in 1959 when the large infants' classroom was converted, along with the adjoining classroom, into a school kitchen and dining hall. These substantial changes were made possible because it was then that all the children over the age of 11 transferred to Trewirgie County Secondary School at Redruth.

At the time of writing these pupils go to the Redruth Community School. Stithians County Primary School was among the first primary schools in Cornwall to have access to the internet. Now, as we approach the millennium, all of the classes in the school are *au fait* with computers and each class has its own e-mail address.

Stithians Boys' School, c.1903. Mr J. Kelynack was the headmaster. William John Pascoe is in the front row, far left. Benjamin John (Bennie) Corey is second from the right in the 3rd row.

The school in c.1908.
Leslie Collins and Bryant Woodward Knuckey are somewhere in the second row.
Alfred Duff is third from the left in the front row.
Note the hob-nailed boots all along the front row of boys!

SCHOOL DAYS

Stithians schoolgirls, 1914.
Centre: fourth from the left, Gwennie Manhire; front: far left, Lily Cock, 5th from the left, Olive Peters, 7th from the left, Liley May Dunstan, 8th from the left, Doris Bolitho, 9th from the left, Myra Glencoe Choak.

Infants Class, 1914, teacher, Miss Lottie Jane Allen.
Back: far left, ? Terrill, 6th from the left, Harold Collins;
centre: far left, Winston Knuckey, 3rd from the left, Netta Dunstan, 6th from the left, Ray Berryman, 8th from the left, Mary Porter, 9th from the left, Hazel Reed;
front: far left, Lilla Collins, 5th from the left, Claude Martin (holding slate).

The Dairy School in front of Crellow House, 1914. Holding the notice is Winifred Jane Corey, one of the students there. The tall, bowler-hatted gentleman at the rear is, possibly, Mr Ernie Andrew of Sewrah Mill.

SCHOOL DAYS

Group of teachers, c.1915.
Left to right, back: M. Hicks and Alma Hicks (sisters), ?, J. Allen and M.A. Allen (sisters); front: J. Gluyas, ?, L. Gluyas (sister of J. Gluyas).

The boys of Stithians School in militant mood on parade with their wooden swords, 1915.

Above: *Stithians School, early 1920s. Left to right, back: Muriel Bolitho, Avis Martin, Ivy War, Olive Bowden, Violet Collins, Gwen Burley, Clarice Collins, Nellie Rodda; 3rd row: Leonard Knuckey, Leslie Odgers, Gwennie Sincock, Una Andrew, Elsie Peters, Will Pascoe, Howard Phillips; 2nd row: Peter Hearne, Creswell Spargo, ? Butlin, Seymour Trevena, Edgar Phillips, Willie Collins; front: Kenneth Harris, Morley Trerise.*

Above: *Stithians School, Standard Three, 1921, with their teacher, Miss Helen Hellings.*

Right: *Schoolchildren, c.1925. Left to right, back: ?, ?, ?, Norman Williams, ? Tresidder, ?, Garfield Eddy, ?; front: ?, Jack Jolly, Fred Dunstan, ?, ?, ?, ?.*

SCHOOL DAYS

Stithians Infants, c.1928.
Left to right, back: Aubrey Curnow, Jack Kemp, Jack Martin, Ivan Dower, Frank Tresidder, Wallace Williams, Fred Dunstan;
centre: Betty Gluyas, Patsy Benney, ? White, Janie Bowden, Dorothy Bath, Joyce Firbanks, Jean Duff, Ethel Thomas;
front: ?, Nancy Martin, Eileen Kemp, Percival Duff, Audrey Phillips, Sheila Sanders.

Stithians Infants, c.1929.
Left to right, back: Pauline Andrew, Kathleen Burleigh, John Thomas, Clifford Williams, Tom Penaluna, ?, Dorothy Thomas, ?;
centre: Marion Dunstan, Betty Moore, ? Johns, Doris Burleigh, Edna Burley, ?, Ivy Rule, ? Jeffrey;
front: Clara Triggs, Leila Ford, Eric Temby, Andrew (Sonny) Woolcock, Joyce Reed, Chrissie Triggs.

Left: *Stithians schoolchildren, 1930. Left to right, back: Gordon Hall, Brian Corey, ?, Miriam Dower, Marian Mitchell, ?, ?, ?, Millie Burley, Andrew (Sonny) Woolcock; centre: ?, Noel Ford, ?, Barbara Williams, Arnold Knuckey, Betty Moore, Eric Temby, ?, Ronald Webber, ?; front: ?, ?, Ruth Phillips, Peter and Peggy Phillips, (twins), ?, ?.*

Above: *Collins House, winners on Sports Day, 1938. Left to right, back: Ralph Berryman, Henry Nicholas, Ronald Webber; 3rd row: Rita Webber, Alison Corey, Audrey Tremayne; 2nd row: Roy Mitchell, Barbara Williams, Kenneth Reynolds, Marion Williams; front: Winston Tremayne, Peter Phillips.*

Left: *Teachers of the early 1930s. Left to right: Miss Una Andrew, Miss Edwards (seated), Miss E.M. Henderson.*

Right: *Stithians schoolchildren, c.1933. Left to right, back: ?, Muriel Toy, ? Goldsworthy, Joyce Reed, Thelma Rowe, Edith Young, Ivy Rule, ?, Marion Dunstan, Arnold Pascoe; centre: Jack Burleigh, Marjorie Bath, Eleanor Williams, Glencoe Dunstan, Bernice Kneebone, Clara and Chrissie Triggs (twins), ?, Percival Duff, Noel Andrew; front: Kenneth Reynolds, Andrew (Sonny) Woolcock, Arnold Burley, ?, Fred Dunstan, ?, Eddie Brown.*

SCHOOL DAYS

Left: *Stithians Council School, 1935. Left to right, back: Mr Harry Mitchell (headmaster), Jack Simmons, Bobby Trerise, Edgar Kemp, Percival Duff, Vivian Downing, Bernard Martin; front: Gordon Hall, Kenneth Reynolds, Lawrence Burley, Glenwood Odgers, Russell Pascoe, John Thomas, Jack Knuckey.*

Right: *Stithians Infants School, Class I, 1935. Left to right, back: Miss J. Hellings (teacher), Henry Penna, Jack Manhire, Dennis Cossentine, Couldrey Martin, Hubert Burley, Peter Moore, Roy Trerise; centre: Marjorie Berryman, Gillian Collins, Eileen Strick, Bernice Nicholls, Daphne Dunstan, Doreen Penna, Marion Prowse; front: Mervyn Pascoe, Rex Collins, William Prowse, ?.*

Left: *Standard I, 1937. Left to right, back: Morris Martin, Arthur Burley, Ivan Perry, Brian Jeffrey, Ralph Berryman, Donald Nicholas, Dudley Kneebone, Dennis Vivian; front: Roy Mitchell, John Williams, Douglas Burley, Alison Corey, Audrey Tremayne, Rosemary Prowse, Lorna Bache.*

Right: *Class I, 1936. Left to right, back: Miss J. Hellings (teacher), Cecil Keverne, John Williams, Pearl Drew, Pauline Collins, Mamie Richards, Joyce Green, John Knuckey, Ralph Berryman; 3rd row: Rosemary Prowse, Lorna Bache, Audrey Tremayne, Alison Corey, Rita Webber, Doreen Penna, Daphne Dunstan, Marion Prowse; 2nd row: Donald Nicholas, Desmond Burley, Dennis Vivian, Thornleigh Dunstan, Orlando Keverne, Douglas Burley, Couldrey Martin; front: Ivan Perry, Roy Mitchell, Dudley Kneebone.*

Left: *The Pied Piper of Hamelin, performed by the schoolchildren in honour of headmaster Mr Harry Mitchell's retirement, 1947. Left to right, back: Lucille Combellack, Heather Winn, Eric Trerise, John Bache, Dawn Thomas, Tony Mair, Mary Clemens, Gwen Pascoe, Shirley Thomas, Pamela Thomas; centre, Alan Collins, Elizabeth (Lee) Prowse, Pat Mair, Gloria Stapleton, Michael Andrew; front: Barry Thomas, Betty King, Frank Andrew.*

Right: *The special occasion of 19 November 1947 – the eve of HRH, Princess Elizabeth's wedding.*

Stithians School Girls' Choir, 1947, with headmaster, Mr Rex Hart.
Left to right, back: Valerie Collins, Betty Gilkes, Marlene Eddy, Valerie Joyce Collins, Jessie Smillie, Christine Andrew, Marjorie Julian, Olive Stribley, Grace Roberts, Margaret Bowden, Kathleen Clemens; centre: Lucille Combellack, Heather Dunstan, Dawn Thomas, Jean Bowden, Enid Waters, Carol Pitts, Shirley Thomas, Betty King, Gloria Stapleton;
front: Benita King, Margaret Waters, Lee Bowden, Jean Allard, Marlow Pascoe, Pamela Thomas, Mary Clemens, Roberta Tresidder.

SCHOOL DAYS

Left: *The retirement of Miss Janie Hellings, 28 September 1945. Miss Hellings is seen here being presented with a cheque by the head girl. Miss Hellings had been a scholar and teacher at Stithians School for 60 years. Left to right: the vicar, the Revd G. Hanley, Mr W.J.T. Peters (Chairman of Managers), Rosemary Downing (head girl), Mr F. Hayman (District Clerk), Miss Janie Hellings, Mr Harry Mitchell (headmaster).*

Right: *The retirement of headmaster, Mr Harry Mitchell, 1947. Left to right: Miss Edwards, Marjorie Julian (head girl), Mrs Tombs, Pastor Buckley, Miss Janie Hellings (retired head of the infants), Mr Harry Mitchell and Mrs Mitchell, Mr W.J.T Peters and Mrs Ethyl Andrew (of the Managers), Mrs E.M. Phillips.*

Left: *On 19 December 1957, the head girl, Mary James, was presented with a necklace by the headmaster, Mr Jack R. Williams. Mary had achieved something quite unique – she had attended school at Stithians for ten years (throughout her entire school life), without having had a single day away. She is seen here wearing her necklace and being congratulated by Mr Williams.*

Below: *Stithians CP School, 1958, with headmaster, Mr J.R. Williams, and Mrs E.M. Phillips.*

Stithians School Infants, 1961.
Left to right, back: Miss Connie Read, Treve Williams, Ann Drew, ?, Carole Dolton, ?, Joy Penaluna; front: Barry Collins, David Phillips, Bridget Prowse, Sarah ?, Steven May, Susan Trerise, John Corey, Stephen Tremayne, Leslie Pascoe, Jane Burleigh, Graham Martin.

Stithians School Infants, 1964.
Left to right, back: Steven May, Leslie Pascoe, Peter Williams, John Corey, Stephen Tremayne, Raymonde Reeve; centre: Treve Williams, Jane Burleigh, Susan Davies, Carol Dolton, Susan Richards, Graham Martin, Bridget Prowse; front: Caroline Pascoe, David Phillips, Elaine Burley, Vanessa Clark, Barry Collins, Susan Trerise, Felicity Prowse, Ronald Thomas, Peter Wojciechowski, Mandy Webber.

SCHOOL DAYS

Stithians School, class 1, 1999. Left to right, back: Scott Trerise, Nigel Ingram, Jenny Fowler-Upton, Gemma Clarke, Jessica Hampton;
centre: Lauren Blee, Jonathan Ward, Keith Hill, Steven Farrell, Darrel Smith, Colin Rool, Mr J.N. Seth (who has been at the school for 21 years and is, in 1999, deputy headmaster);
front: Michelle Laity, Jamie Tait, Hayley Rowe, Robert Crooke, Emma Rodwell, Nathan Cook, Tom Semmens, Charlotte Rashleigh.

Left: 'Special Award for the best Work of Art', awarded to Charlotte Rashleigh, aged 9, of Stithians School, for her drawing entitled 'My House'. The award was made as part of the 1998 'Award to Cornish Schools for Studies of the Environment'. This competition was organised by the Royal Institute of British Architects (Cornwall Branch), and was sponsored jointly by ECC International, Europe, the Design Bureau and Cornwall Education Business Partnership.

St Stithians College in its beautiful parkland setting of 240 acres.

The imposing interior of the chapel and (inset) *the bronze tablet commemorating the founders.*

Chapter 8: St Stithians College

Two Cornishmen, Albert John Collins born in Stithians in 1859, and William Mountstephens born in the same year at Falmouth, formed a life-long friendship when they became colleagues as apprentices in the building trade in William Mountstephens' home town in the late 1870s. In common with many men of the time they determined to improve their prospects and travelled to Johannesburg, South Africa, where, over the years, they became extremely wealthy businessmen. Imbued with concern for the wellbeing of others, the partners distributed vast funds to numerous organisations charged with the care of the disadvantaged; their generosity embraced every part of the community in the city they had come to regard as home

Albert Collins and William Mountstephens had a great desire to endow an establishment of permanent benefit to Johannesburg and after much deliberation agreed that the residues of their estates would be used to found a private school. Arrangements were made for the setting up of a trust fund with the firm directive that the proposed school would be controlled by the Methodist Church. Many years later the Chairman of the College Council, the Revd Stanley Pitts, wrote of such a school being the 'realisation of the hopes and dreams of a number of people who, over the years, had longed to see a Methodist school which would serve the Transvaal as Kingswood and Kearsney had served the Cape and Natal'. He also referred to the initial difficulty in that 'those who felt keenly the need of such a school had not the funds to build it – while those who possessed the funds were not persuaded of the need (referring to Albert Collins and William Mountstephens)'. Both men contributed generously to orphanages and hospitals, both in South Africa and in their home county of Cornwall, but education was looked on as the task of the State. It was only when state schools came to be regarded as concentrating too exclusively on the academic side of education, to the detriment of the cultivation of the spirit, that the possibility of establishing a Methodist Church school, which would place greater emphasis on the teaching of Christian faith and practice, was seriously considered. It was then that Messrs Collins and Mountstephens decided to make their bequest. Albert Collins died in 1937 and, his large estate having been distributed, the Methodist Conference was empowered to appoint trustees. They were the Revd E. Bottrill, Chairman of the Transvaal and Swaziland District of the Methodist Church, Messrs C.H. Leake and C.K. Tucker, executors of the estate, and Mr D.F. Corlett, a former Mayor of Johannesburg and Chairman of the United Building Society of South Africa. The first meeting took place on 4 February 1941 and was attended by Mr William Mountstephens. He proposed the name of the St Stithians Trust which was accepted.

St Stithians College Chapel.

In succeeding years the name became associated with the planned school and although a formal meeting was held in 1952 to decide what it would be called, the name St Stithians College had become an accepted term and was adopted (despite some admitting problems with pronunciation and spelling). William Mountstephens participated in arrangements for the purchase of the land and was involved in discussions about the management of the school at the time of his own death in 1943. His widow, Mrs S. Mountstephens, went to live in Cape Town.

The Trust meeting of November 1941 resolved to purchase land forming part of Driefontein Farm in No. 3 District of Johannesburg at a total cost of £8713.5s.0d. Situated on the borders of the northern suburbs of Bryanston and Ferndale, the property was less than ten miles from the centre of Johannesburg. In 1944 architects were appointed and a firm of consulting engineers drew up plans for the playing field, drainage and roads for which a contract was signed in 1946. July 1947 saw the submission of the plan for the building and estimates were sought with the following options:

Full scheme for 500 pupils   £427 970
A scheme for 200 pupils   £196 000

The revenue from both estates was as follows:

Albert Charles Collins	*£166 838*
William Mountstephens	*£188 415*
Total	*£355 253*

The trustees faced a major decision about the right time to build. The anticipated drop in building costs at the end of the Second World War did not materialise; there was also additional pressure to stem the deterioration of the site works already in place. Thus the trustees agreed to go ahead in 1950. Inevitably new estimates were necessary and taking practical and financial constraints into account the trustees confirmed the commencement of a school for 100 pupils with the intention of opening the establishment in 1953.

Initially it was intended that the assembly hall would be built first and the chapel later on. However, to the great pleasure of the trustees, a recommendation was made to the effect that the chapel – destined as the nucleus of the school – should be erected on the site intended for the hall.

St Stithians College opened on Wednesday 28 January 1953 with 84 pupils; the boarders were accommodated in Collins House. The full-time members of staff were Mr W.G.A. Mears, headmaster, Miss Ann Doehring, Miss Betty Walmsley, Mr E.N. Harris and two part-time staff. Building operations delayed the formal opening and the great day arrived on 3 February 1953 with a service of dedication in the presence of about 150 people. Dr J.B. Webb, Chairman of the Transvaal and Swaziland Methodist District, opened the service bringing greetings from Kingswood, Kearsney and Epworth Methodist Schools. There was a telegram from Mrs W. Mountstephens expressing her good wishes and congratulations.

At last the laying of the chapel's foundation stone arrived. A gathering of over 700 included members of the European Synod, representatives of the three Methodist schools and other churches, the Salvation Army and the Cornish Association. Bishop Reeves of Johannesburg and Dr J.B. Webb were the principal speakers and the Chairman of the College Council, Mr G.K. Tucker (an executor, with Mr C.H. Leake, JP, of Albert Collins' Estate) paid tribute to the founders of the college. Dr J.B. Webb declared the college open and the foundation stone was laid by Mr C.H. Leake, JP.

> THIS STONE WAS LAID ON THE
> ELEVENTH DAY OF AUGUST 1953
> TO MARK THE HAPPY FULFILMENT
> OF A TRUST TO ESTABLISH THIS
> COLLEGE IN THE NAME OF THE
> METHODIST CHURCH
>
> TRUSTEES
> D.F. CORLETT   C.H. LEAKE
> G.K. TUCKER   J.B. WEBB

Mrs S. Mountstephens unveiled the bronze tablet appropriately placed in the area linking classrooms and the chapel. This special day concluded with the presentation of a silver trophy by the Transvaal Cornishmen's Association in memory of the founders. From that day, 11 August became Founders' Day and its anniversary has been celebrated ever since. A few months later a distinctive entrance was completed at the roadside; built in gold-coloured brick, it was identified as the Corlett Gateway, a tribute to Mr D.F. Corlett, a trustee.

The completion of Mountstephens House ensured that more boarders were in residence by January 1954. The chapel was opened on Sunday 7 November 1954 and its 700 seats were soon taken; worshippers lined the walls and others listened from the doors whilst the pupils were accommodated sitting on the floor in front of the

The chapel window depicting the Good Samaritan.

congregation and in the aisles. This impressive gathering was brought to a close with the full choir of the Methodist Central Hall singing 'Te Deum Laudamas'.

The first celebration of Founders' Day took place at morning assembly in August 1954 when the headmaster gave a summary of the history of the college. Further anniversaries assumed a formal style in the chapel with a guest speaker and support from soloists, choirs, parents and – as the years sped by – Old Boys too. Ministers and preachers from the Central Methodist Hall took Sunday services from 1953-54 and in 1955 the Revd Vivian Harris became the first chaplain. Gifts flowed in to further enhance the interior of the chapel, including a stained-glass window (*opposite below*), a red and gold pulpit cloth and carved oak chairs, each in memory of loved ones. Mr G.K. Tucker, ever supportive, gave the organ and the Parents' Association provided the vestry furniture.

In 1986 Mr M. Henning, the then headmaster, wrote to the author:

We enjoy our old and tenuous link with Cornwall and are often surprised by how many of our school families make a pilgrimage to the birthplace of our founders.

St Stithians College has gained a formidable reputation academically, culturally, and in the sphere of sport. Ever innovative 'Saints' embarked on a second foundation and in January 1995 St Stithians Collegiate for Girls was established and has proved a resounding success. The schools remain separate, each retaining its own identity, but with equal opportunities and the advantages of learning and sharing with each other.

In 1998 189 candidates passed the Matriculation Examinations with no failures. House names include Collins, Mountstephens, Penryn, Pitts, Tucker, Webb and Wesley with friendly rivalry between them.

The Duke of Cornwall Singers comprises 15 members led by Mrs O. Hoogenhout. Their programme is busy and varied and has included performances in chapels, for the Tourism Board and the Nelson Mandela Children's Fund at the Presidential residence. A tour of Natal was successful and the 'Dukes' augmented their funds by singing at weddings, which enabled them to record a CD in 1998. Their annual report indicated that they were pleased with their progress when they remarked:

The way the girls at a Collegiate screamed when member Thomas threw his blazer over his shoulder in 'Goodnight Sweetheart' and chased him to the bus after the show, asking for his phone number, will always be remembered.

Mr David Wylde's report on Speech Day last year gives us a peep into college tradition. He drew from the winning poem 'My St Stithians' (based on a theme of permanence) and gave an example of what is permanent at Saints – from the final matric assembly. The matrics sat in the pews at the front of the chapel, a change from their normal place in the gallery. On the day all other grades move back in the chapel with Grade II in the gallery. They have progressed in seniority so there is an air of expectation on the day. Grades 8 to 11 are each represented by one boy who pays tribute to the matrics – sometimes in a touching and dignified way, or in an amusing, revealing speech. The 'Dukes' sing, the musicians play, then they end with the college song during which the matrics file out of the back of the chapel, many emotional with tears in their eyes (*below*). The pews they have occupied are vacant. There is a hole in the front of the chapel; those left behind are pretty wide-eyed at this symbol – a visible departing. The organ stops playing. There is silence in the chapel but for those who know what is happening one can pick up the slight sound of scuffling outside and then there comes the sound of the war cry – 'Oh when the saints... ' and stamping from the matrics outside on the chapel circle. It's enough to make your hair stand on end!

The following year, at the first assembly, the vacated seats remain empty until the new Grade 8 files into the pews. When they have arrived the college bursts into spontaneous applause. The baton has been passed on.

In 1999 the college has 2282 pupils of which 150 of the senior boys are boarders. In 2003 the college will have half a century of achievement to celebrate. Long may the saints go marching in... St Stithians, we salute you and send you our very best wishes.

John Collins enlisted into the Army (against his father's wishes and possibly under age) during the First World War. He went away with his brother-in-law and both men lost their lives.

Chapter 9: In Times of War

Boer War

William was the great-grandson of James and Catherine Martin of Crellow House and Thomas and Elizabeth Spargo of Trebost. He was also the grand uncle of the author of this piece, Janet Ivey. He was born in 1845 at Crellow, Stithians, and was a foreman gunpowder maker in the Kennall Vale Works until his sight was damaged in an explosion in the early 1880s and emphysema was taking its toll. William and his wife, Mary Amanda (née Thomas), with their three sons and six daughters, moved into Half Moon House where William turned to the occupation of innkeeper.

Tragedy touched the lives of all three of the couple's sons. In March 1882, John (then 17 months of age), was killed outright by a pony and cart just outside Half Moon House, and by the following Christmas his mother was dead. Brothers William, born 1869, and Solomon, ten years younger, journeyed to South Africa to seek work in the mines. Their father died in 1894 and the daughters received the dreadful news in August 1899 that Solomon had lost his life in a mining accident.

Many Cornishmen were involved in the Boer War (1899-1902) and William had served 186 days in another battalion before enlisting as a Kitchener Fighting Scout on 17 July 1901. Tragically William perished several weeks later in August 1901 aged only 32 years. He was unmarried. William's death signalled the end of a branch of the Spargo family which had been associated with Trebost for several centuries. Parishes were asked to remember the fallen by installing memorials, such as brass plates, in their churches. In March 1905 a memorial service was held in Truro Cathedral. The Earl of Mount Edgcumbe, Lord Lieutenant of Cornwall, unveiled the monument erected in memory of officers and men of the County Regiment and all Cornish men who lost their lives in the South-African War.

The monument which is attached to the wall of the south-west tower is of slightly polished polyphant stone, is about 10 feet high and nearly 15 feet long. Above a plain base, 3 feet high, is a canopied panel containing the Cornish arms, motto and the inscription:

Sacred to the memory of the officers and men of the County Regiment and all Cornishmen who died for their Country in South Africa 1899-1902.

William Spargo is remembered in the cathedral of his county and he lies in the peace of Fort Napier Cemetery in Pietermaritzburg where his comrades laid him to rest. The grave is marked with an aluminium cross.

The Church of England cemetery is carefully tended by the War Graves Commission. *Requiescat in pace.*

Half Moon House.

Left: *During the First World War Miss Janie Hellings was very much involved in the production of concerts in the Village Hall. These concerts were organised to raise funds for the boys at the front line. Miss Hellings herself took part in song and dance routines with her young niece, Ruby Martin, who would have been, perhaps, seven or eight years of age at the time. The pair are seen in this photograph performing one of their dance routines.*

Right: *The First-Aid Post, Stithians Vicarage. Left to right, back: Sadie Porter, Joyce Andrew, Mrs R. Richards, Mrs Florence Wills, Mrs Moyle, Doris Downing, Miss Hellings, Mrs Kirk; front: Margaret Kirk, June Gardner, Doreen Toy, Leila Ford, Mrs G. Spargo. Sunday afternoons were very often spent going out to mock aeroplane crashes and other similar incidents.*

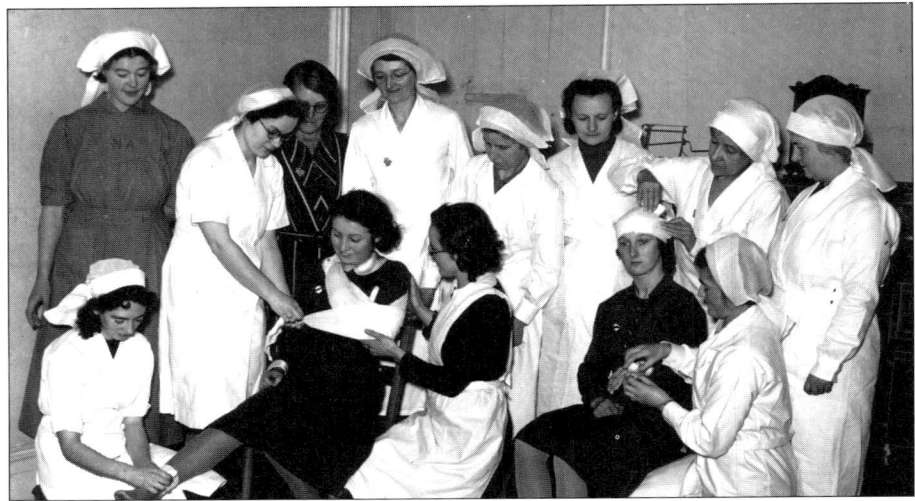

Left: *A soup kitchen at an outbuilding at Tregonning Mill during the Second World War, organised by the ladies of the Stithians branch of the Women's Voluntary Service. Miss Hellings can be seen in the foreground, to the left.*

IN TIMES OF WAR

First and Second World Wars

Several concerts were held in the church schoolroom in aid of the National Relief Fund during the early part of the First World War and the children were trained by Jane and Helen Hellings. A total of £35 was raised.

A Belgian relief committee, formed after a meeting held on 15 January 1915, decided to host a Belgian family in the parish and on 16 February 1915 a Belgian family of four, plus an adult niece, arrived in Stithians. They were housed in a cottage free of rent and furnished from proceeds of several more concerts. Yet another concert raised £3 and was donated to the Fund for the 'Suffering Serbians'.

Much to everyone's surprise (those who saw it, that is), one Sunday at midday during the First World War, a Zeppelin airship came into view over Crellow Hill. The incident was duly reported to the authorities at Falmouth.

On 3 September 1939 Neville Chamberlain announced, 'We are at war with Germany'. Life would never be the same again for anyone. For two years a small group of women had been learning and practising first aid in a room which then became an air-raid post. The Reverend Kirk, vicar of Stithians at the time, with his wife and daughter Margaret, were members of this group, who were almost all members of the St John's Ambulance Brigade as well. Working and liaising with the Air Raid Wardens, who would have been the first group to receive an air-raid warning, the group was under the charge of Mrs F. Wills of Pencoose.

A German Luftwaffe bomber flew low over the village and Miss Hellings, head of the junior school, took all her pupils to the safety of the vicarage where there were plenty of trees for cover. However, the pilot had other plans and carried on to Falmouth where he unloaded his bombs and took the town completely by surprise, so much so that not one anti-aircraft gun was fired. It was then that barrage balloons were placed in all the strategic positions over town and harbour.

Fifteen incendiary bombs were dropped on Stithians during the night of 21 May 1941. Six bullocks and a pig were killed and four houses at Goonlaze damaged. One of the bombs had dropped among eight cows owned by Mr Tripp of Tresevern and these animals (constituting his entire herd) later had to be put down under veterinary supervision.

Miss Janie Hellings formed a National Savings group and was responsible for collecting over £44 000 from the year 1917. For this she was awarded the British Empire Medal. The Women's Institute formed a Wartime Produce Guild and produced over 5000lbs of jam which was then sold to parishioners.

Kathleen Robinson (on the left), evacuee billeted with Mr and Mrs E.E. Perry of Trebarveth Farm, helping Joan Perry (the farmer's daughter) to plant potatoes.

June 1940 brought the first batch of evacuees to the parish. Mrs Gordon, wife of Colonel Gordon of Trevales, was the billeting officer helped by all Women's Institute members. Another batch of evacuees arrived in October 1940. One young lad, Dennis Parsons, was among this group of children and related, during a recent visit to the village, how he had climbed over the rubble created by the previous night's air raid on his home area. The next day his parents took him to his school where he bid them farewell and, with his small suitcase and gas mask, he boarded a coach for Paddington. He was nine years of age, and even though he was with his classmates and his friends from his East Ham school, it still must have been a very traumatic experience for him and all of the children.

At first, Dennis was billeted with Mrs Collins in Crellow Lane (along with three other boys), and later moved to be with Mr and Mrs W. Andrew at Ennis and Carbis Farm. He says that these were some of the happiest days of his boyhood. He had come from a very poor family and was quite spoiled by Mrs Andrew who had no children of her own. Dennis enjoyed the farm life and was taught to milk a cow and to ride a horse so that when the horse needed shoeing he was set upon its back to ride to the farrier at Foundry.

At this time Mr Harry Mitchell was the headmaster of Stithians School which was full to overflowing. Some of the London school's teaching staff had come with the evacuees and taught their own classes in the same rooms alongside the Stithians children. Miss Hellings, head of the junior school, lived quite close to the school and to Ennis and Carbis. She asked Dennis Parsons to draw off a pitcher of water from the village pump each day for her own household and for this he received a sixpenny National Savings stamp at the rate of one per week. At the end of 30 weeks

A group of evacuees with some local children. The picture was taken in August 1941 at a garden fête held in the grounds of Crellow House. It was here that many of the evacuees were billeted, the house having been taken over specifically for that purpose.

Above: *More evacuees, this time at Tregonning Mill, emulating 'Old Uncle Tom Cobley and all', c.1941. Standing is Peggy Phillips, third daughter of Mr and Mrs Aubrey Phillips of Tregonning Mill.*

Left: *Dennis Parsons, an evacuee from the London area.*

Dennis received a 15-shilling National Savings Certificate. If he kept it for five years the accumulated interest would have made his 15 shillings into £1 (and this, so Dennis says, was his introduction to the idea of money saving). Quite a few of the evacuees kept in touch with their temporary foster parents after the war.

The parish was host to American troops during the run-up to the D-Day landings in 1944, as well as to the Women's Land Army. There was also a lively contingent of the Local Defence Volunteers (later the Home Guard). At first, their uniform was just an armband bearing the letters LDV, with tin helmets and boots completing the ensemble. Their weapons were broomsticks! Later, full uniform became a khaki blouson and trousers and regulation boots. They were also equipped with rifles and bayonets. Mr Bishop-Stevens (Perran-ar-Worthal) was their Commander-in-Chief with Major Perry of Trebarveth next in command. An observation post at Cascadden in 1940 and a searchlight battery at Higher Tremenhere Farm, as well as another, later, at Little Plymouth, made up the parish defences.

On 16 April 1941 a Bristol Blenheim MK IV, serial No: V5518, of 53 Squadron, Coastal Command, crashed at Trolvis. Pilot Officer R.C.L. Reade and Observer Sergeant J.D. O'Connell were both killed. WOP/AG Sergeant R.H. Camm was the sole survivor (*opposite, inset*). Oscar Peters and Kitchener Young (*opposite, main picture*), both of Stithians, were first on the scene and pulled Sergeant Camm clear from the plane at great personal risk to themselves. They saved his life by their gallantry and were later summoned to Buckingham Palace to be presented with meritorious awards, medals and certificates.

Right: *The War Memorial outside St Stythians Parish Church.*

The Perry family in front of their farmhouse at Trebarveth. Left to right, back: Edward Perry (elder son), Major E.E. Perry (Stithians Home Guard), Ivan Perry; front: Mrs Perry and daughter Joan.

Longdowns Home Guard (No. 2 Platoon, 7th Battalion, DCLI Stithians Division) (photograph taken by Commanding Officer, Captain Richard Rowe).
Left to right, back (privates): W. Opie, J. Hearne, G. Williams, B. Green, A. Tarrant, R. Nicholls, C. Bonney, J. Medlyn, J. King, W. Evans, H. Rashleigh, P. Bolitho, W. Dunstan, S. Hearne;
centre: W. Warr, L. Wills, L. Trewhella, A. Duff, W. Winn, A. Trewhella, J. Lavers, A. Rogers, E. Trewhella, S. Matthews, E. Trewhella, W. Hosken, W. Lawrence; front: Cpl. A. Spargo, Cpl G. Oppy, Sgt G. Richards, 2nd Lt. W. Oppy, Lt. F. Williams, Platoon Sgt. A. Opie, Cpl R. Polkinhorne, W. Cox.

Section of Stithians Home Guard, 1941, photographed at the entrance to the Vicarage.
Left to right, back: S. Terrill, G. Stribley, ?, Douglas Moyle, J.D. Pascoe, C. Spargo, E.E. Perry, T.H. Stribley, A.J. Ford, L.H. Burleigh, Revd Perry, Cecil Mead, B. Moyle, T.J. Andrew, D. Pascoe, J. Knuckey, N. Tregenza;
front: Harold Phillips, Ray Berryman, P. Duff, Mr Botton, Bill Botton, Roger Polkinhorn, W. Odgers, Wilfred Prowse, F. Duff, J.H. Burleigh, C. Knuckey.
Despatch rider, Eric Temby. The little boy standing so proudly beside him is Brian Prowse.

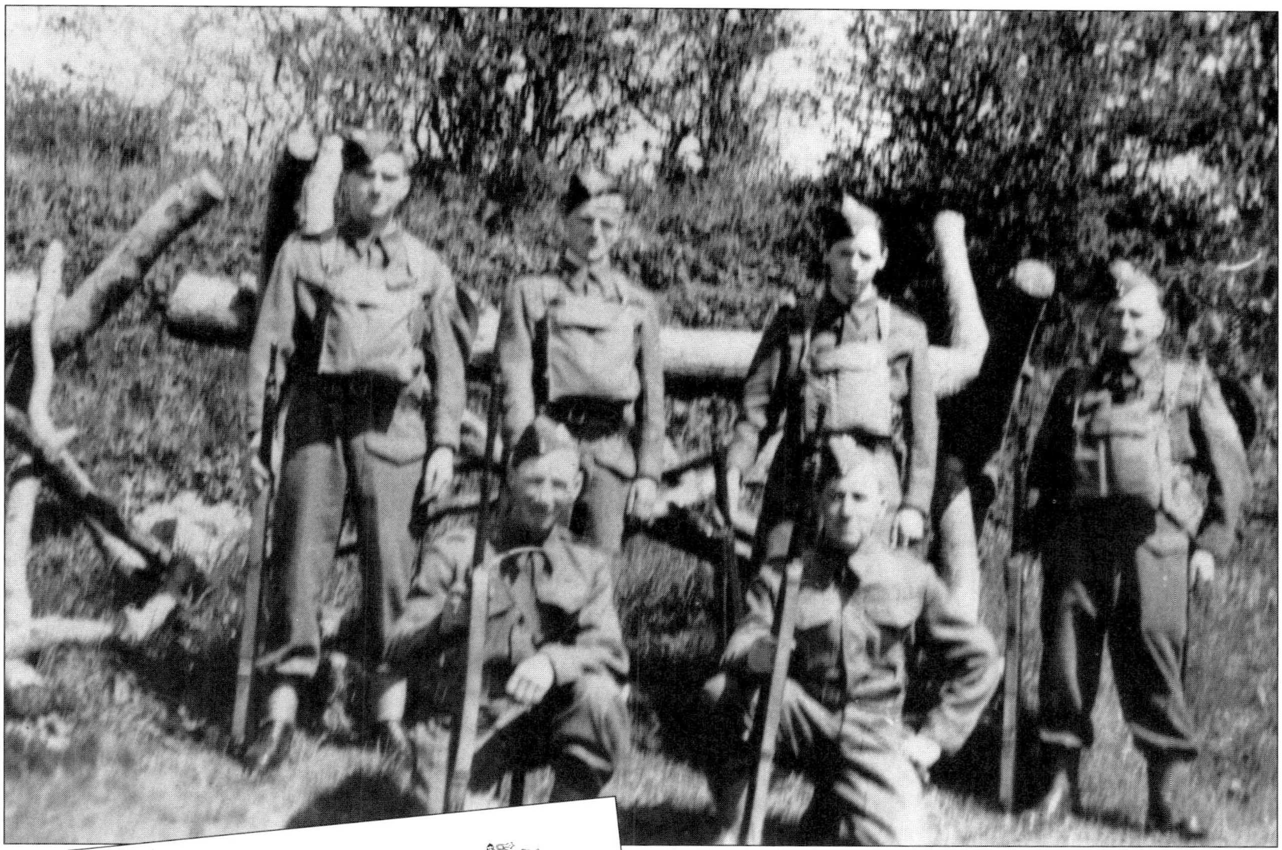

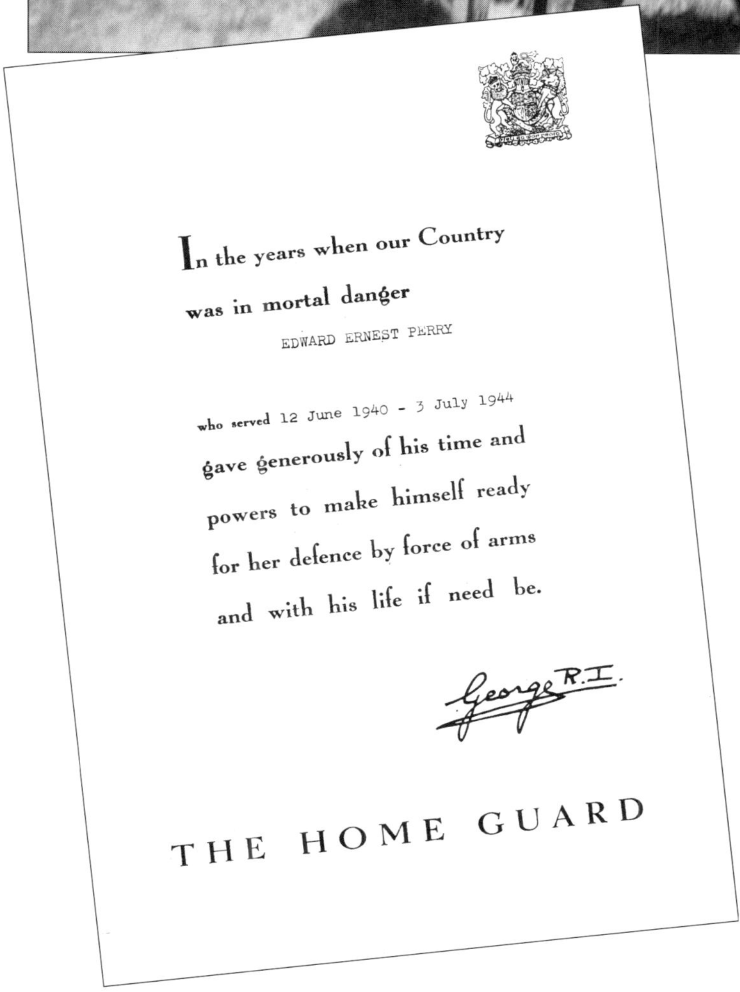

In the years when our Country
was in mortal danger
EDWARD ERNEST PERRY
who served 12 June 1940 - 3 July 1944
gave generously of his time and
powers to make himself ready
for her defence by force of arms
and with his life if need be.

George R.I.

THE HOME GUARD

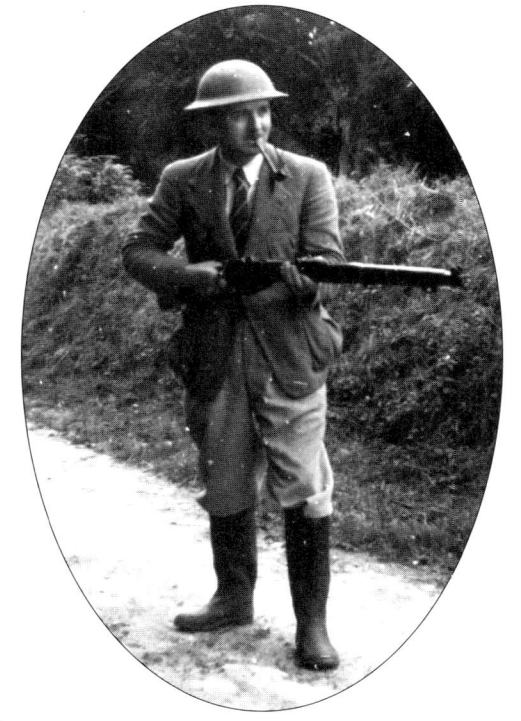

Top: *Barricades set up at the top of Little Plymouth Hill. Left to right, back: R. Dunstan, J. Pascoe, E. Perry, Sgt Moore; front: W. Burley, C. Spargo.*

Above: *Major E.E. Perry (of the Home Guard) at Trebarveth Farm, where he resided at that time and* (left) *the award presented to him from HM King George, for services rendered.*

Top: *The base of the Wellington monument on its journey from Longdowns to Reading, 1864.*
Above: *Men from what is thought to be Carncrees Quarry, date unknown.*

Chapter 10: Quarrying

Not only is granite a hard stone but it is also a hard taskmaster. The quarrying and cutting of granite is a great art and one which should never be allowed to die. Such thoughts were addressed to the Cornish and Devon Granite Masters Association in 1947 by Lt. Col. E.H. Bolitho, CB, DSO, Lord Lieutenant and Chairman of Cornwall County Council. He continued with his hope that granite would again be used in the construction of buildings of dignity and importance and also in the preparation of memorials 'for which latter purpose there is no finer stone'.

Doubt has been expressed as to whether there is a material which gives nobler effects, is more durable or lends itself so well to the speedy execution of large works as does Cornish granite. The great megalithic monuments in Cornwall are the first granite structures. The Cornish wayside crosses, at least as early as 8th-century, were created from grass rock, the basic form which had lain on the ground exposed to the elements for thousands of years.

Stone in the parish has been used since earliest times and the granite industry itself came into being in the middle of the 18th century, principally in the Constantine area. There is a record of large quantities of moorstone from Stithians, Mabe and Constantine being shipped from Penryn at the beginning of the 19th century. By 1854 Stithians was acknowledged for the production of 'vast quantities of granite which was shipped for London and other places, to be used for buildings, bridges and quays'. There were quarries at varying times at Carncrees, Chywoon, Herniss Yards, Kennall Vale, Lower Trolvis, Old Trolvis, Polkannuggo, Rosemanowes, Tresevern, Trevales and Trolvis. The majority were located close to the Longdowns area.

Quarries are open to the sky and are usually started into the slope of a hill so that if the entrance road is to be continued on the level, the heading of granite becomes higher as the quarry develops. This technique is clearly illustrated in the photographs on the following pages, as at Mabe, Polkanuggo and Carncrees. Most of the granite in Stithians is of the coarse type, plentiful in supply, fairly uniform in texture and composition and with well-developed jointing.

The monumental works of Messrs Richards and Trerise at Point on the Longdowns road.

Extremely large blocks were quarried and a spectacular example was recorded in 1902 when a colossal mass with an estimated weight of 2738 tons was extracted! By way of reinforcement of this enormous achievement at least 70 men gathered on the rock to provide future generations with an arresting record of the event.

Spargo Downs Quarry is a little way over the parish boundary but men from Stithians would have joined the workforce there or married into Mabe families. A large stone was quarried there with a volume of some $465\frac{1}{2}$ cubic feet and an estimated weight of about 38 tons. This large cube was destined to become the base of a monument in memory of the Duke of Wellington on his Strathfield House Estate. The stone was hauled through Longdowns en-route for Penryn Railway Station. This extraordinary load was drawn by 47 horses and it is fortunate indeed that such a feat has been photographically recorded.

Winchester was an important town in Roman times and a centre of great learning in the days of King Alfred's rule (AD871-901). There was a desire to celebrate the King Alfred Millenary but plans were delayed for many reasons, not least because of the hostilities in South Africa (1899-1902). The Guildhall meeting in 1898 approved the proposals for the memorial which comprised two rough-hewn granite monoliths from the quarries of Messrs John Freeman, Sons and Company of Penryn, and specifically from the Trolvis quarry No. 38. The upper monolith when quarried weighed about 54 tons and the lower monolith 48 tons and they were the two largest blocks of granite ever dispatched from the famous quarries of Messrs John Freeman & Company. The two blocks aroused considerable interest whilst in transit. The photographs show the 38 ton die stone being transported in 1901 to Penryn Railway Station and thence to Winchester, completing the journey by road. Every stage of the work which involved risk in raising such immense weights was watched with intense interest by the public in Winchester. When the blocks were raised into their final position 40lb pounds of lump sugar were used to obviate the danger that the block, when pulled up on one edge, might swing beyond the vertical and fall the other way. The sugar slowly

Lower Trolvis, 1947. The group includes, at the back: R. Jenkin, H. Jenkin, W. Pascoe, R. Chegwidden, W. Francis, A. Gay, P. Prisk, G. Francis, E. Winn, J. Martin, A. Dunstan, J. Skinner, J. Caddy, W. James; in the centre: M. Jewell, S. Tregonning, R. Dunstan, H. Francis, H. Martin, A. Prowse, R. Bath, J. Tripp, E. Prisk, J. Bath, W. Dunstan, K. Bowden, J. Pascoe, A. Lloyd, E. Johns, J. Hodge, W. Opie, T. Plummer; at the front: F.R. Simmons, D. Dower, E. Reynolds, E. Penlerick, F. Wise, E. Willoughby.

Above left: *Mr Vivian Downing, c.1947, pictured in the cutting sheds at Kennall Vale. The fronts of the sheds were open in all weathers to minimise the effects of dust.*
Above, centre: *Glenwood Odgers and Tom Penaluna pictured at Kennall, c.1939.*
Above right: *Simon Prisk wields the hammer, watched by Tom Penaluna senr, c.1920s.*

QUARRYING

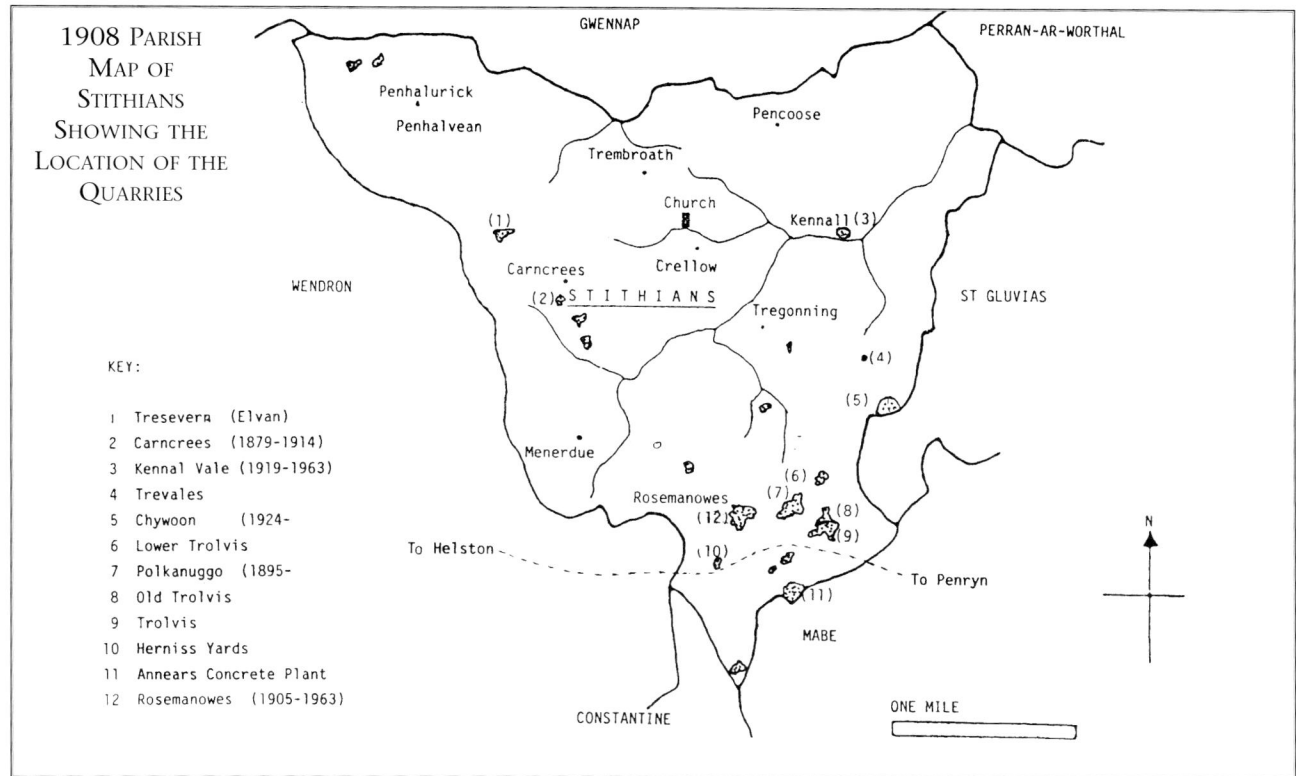

1908 Parish Map of Stithians Showing the Location of the Quarries

KEY:
1. Tresevern (Elvan)
2. Carncrees (1879-1914)
3. Kennal Vale (1919-1963)
4. Trevales
5. Chywoon (1924-
6. Lower Trolvis
7. Polkanuggo (1895-
8. Old Trolvis
9. Trolvis
10. Herniss Yards
11. Annears Concrete Plant
12. Rosemanowes (1905-1963)

disintegrated as it took the great weight and the huge block descended gradually into place. This method was long established although other materials were used later on. A correspondent to a Hampshire newspaper wrote that an acquaintance had the proud memory of standing on top of the block, his father being one of the masons who travelled with it to Winchester.

Carncrees Quarry was trading between 1879 and 1914, initially as Richards and Spargo and subsequently as James A. Richards. Quoins for the Police Station at Redruth (recently vacated) were obtained from Carncrees and were taken to Redruth by Mr Corey who owned the nearby farm. J.A. Richards transferred operations to Kennall Vale where a quarry of fine-grained granite was opened. Mr J.S. Richards continued to trade there, supplying dressed stone for the railway viaducts at Trewedna and Ponsanooth, the latter being the highest viaduct on the Cornish railway, at a height of 140 feet (and a length of 650 feet). The company also worked with other firms to supply stone for the London Embankment as well as constructing war memorials following the First World War.

Once the granite block left the quarry in its rough condition it passed to the mason to be dressed into the finished form. This was highly skilled work and an apprenticeship was essential. Granite does not lend itself to a great deal of ornate treatment but is unsurpassed for monumental, architectural and engineering work. Building work demanded fine measurement so that each stone accurately fitted adjacent stones and precision was also essential in the construction of locks, bridges, coping, steps and kerbs.

Following the First World War Mr Edwin Trerise bought a quarry at Constantine and by 1921 had set up dressing yards at Herniss. The decline in the trade was evident after the Second World War and the business closed in 1966 at the time of Mr Trerise's retirement.

The quarry at Lower Trolvis was taken over by Mr C.E. Ebbutt of Croydon, trading as Western Counties Ltd. and in the 1930s over 100 men were employed there, most of them travelling along the narrow roads from Stithians parish on bicycles. Stone from local quarries was used to build the docks at Grimsby, Devonport and Gibraltar, County Hall in London, Aberystwyth University, National Provincial Bank in Liverpool, Paddington, Cardiff and Swansea Stations, the steps and base of the Eros Statue in Piccadilly, and the South Bank, Putney and Lambeth bridges.

Many men joined the Royal Engineers 853 Company at the outbreak of the Second World War and they quarried stone for the building of airfields at Lisburn, White Mountain in Northern Ireland and Woodstock, Oxford. At the end of the war a training scheme was set up for men coming out of the services so that they could learn the trade.

In 1955 70 men were employed at Lower Trolvis at the time when Mr Alfred C. Prowse became the owner, but the granite industry was in unstoppable decline and in the early 1960s the company closed.

Top: *A very old and faded photograph of Longdowns in 1864 when the momentous load was on its way to Reading. The lead horses and their farmer owners pause to have their photograph taken.*
Above: *Formidable skills were involved in the transportation of the King Alfred Stone in 1898 through Longdowns to Winchester.*

QUARRYING

Top: *This block of granite was dislodged in one piece at Polkanuggo Quarry in 1902. It weighed around 2738 tons and 70 men clambered onto it to help record the event.*
Above: *Group of quarry workers, c.1910, Carncrees Quarry.*

This photograph of Polkanuggo Granite Quarry, carefully posed, c.1885, is an exceptional record of the activities of a quarry in the 19th century and was taken when the steam engine, 'BETA', was purchased. The smithy in the background was used to sharpen tools. (courtesy Royal Institution of Cornwall)

QUARRYING

A head crane in operation, probably at Kennall Quarry, c.1910.

Top: *Messrs J.A. Richards' quarry at Kennall Vale before 1920.*
Above: *This is thought to be Carncrees Quarry, c.1910 – it appears to be crowst time!*

Chapter 11: CSM Geothermal Energy Project

At the south east of the parish is Rosemanowes Quarry, adjacent to Rosemanowes Farm. Quarrying here in 1830 produced some of the finest granite for tombstone memorials and quoins for building projects. The quarry changed ownership several times up to the end of the 19th century and was only worked intermittently during that period. However, towards the end of the century, the viaducts at Ponsanooth and Perran-ar-Worthal were being rebuilt to replace the earlier structures of stone piers and wooden trestles. The work was undertaken by the Great Western Railway Company, supplied with granite quarried from Rosemanowes and extracted by Messrs John Freeman and Company (who were renting the quarry at that time). This was to be, in all probability, the largest single order for granite that the quarry had ever produced.

Then came a lull until the 1920s when a small granite-crushing engine was installed by the Pentewan Dock and Ballast Company. Over the next decade John Freeman and Company was taken over by Messrs McLeod, thus becoming Freeman, McLeod Limited. The next few years saw the quarry again producing granite for memorials and monuments until 1955 when J.C. Annear, a local firm producing concrete blocks, took over. By 1963, however, the type of granite necessary for this work became exhausted leaving a plentiful supply of waste material which had accumulated over the years. This was used as a hard-core and infill for local military establishments and airfields. Simmons Hodge, a local haulage company, was employed to carry out the necessary work.

From 1944 the quarry became a dumping ground, used by the United States Expeditionary Forces, encamped in and around the Stithians area during the period prior to the Normandy landings. Dumping occurred on a daily basis with such provisions as confectionery, fresh fruit, tins of cooked meats and fresh poultry arriving regularly – foods of all kinds that were unobtainable to the British housewife. There were also items of household equipment, including kitchen utensils – the list was endless. Local folk flocked to the quarry every day to glean whatever they could and work in the fields came to a halt as people of all ages, men and women, heard the US army trucks arriving.

At the end of the Second World War, J.C. Annear and Company stripped the eastern end of the quarry of approximately 300 000 tons of stone offcuts and all other wastes and rejects, reducing the whole to a suitable size by first drilling and then 'pop' blasting. Simmons Hodge then transported the rubble to Kessel Downs Quarry ready to be used in the production of ready-mix concrete and other similar commodities.

In 1967 Rosemanowes Quarry ceased to be productive and Penryn Granite (a subsidiary of Selection Trust Limited), acquired the quarrying interests of J.C. Annear.

Above: *Night-time view of the drilling rig.*

Left: *Wellheads and towers in the snow, January 1987.*

Towards the end of 1976, two scientists got together at the quarry to work on a project based on the concept that the deeper one drills down into the Cornish granite the higher the temperature will become. These two men were Dr A.S. Batchelor of the Camborne School of Mines and Dr J. Wheildon of Imperial College, London. Together with Mr Graham Brooks, General Manager of the Penryn Granite Company, they drilled a 142mm diameter hole into the granite at Rosemanowes Quarry to a depth of 196 metres, near the eastern boundary. Other holes were bored and the resultant tests of heat-flow measurements were so successful that, in 1977, the Camborne School of Mines were able to negotiate and obtain a research grant to enable them to investigate the possible geothermal exploitation of this discovery

Dr Batchelor requested permission to drill four boreholes, of 150mm diameter and to a depth of 300 metres in the quarry at Rosemanowes. Thus the Camborne School of Mines (CSM) Geothermal Energy Project (known as 'hotroks') began in earnest.

Two further wells of 2000 metres were drilled, work commencing in August 1981, and then a third well was drilled to a depth of 2600 metres in 1984. A similar project was being operated in Los Alamos, New Mexico; the only other such project in the world. However, drilling there was comparatively easy, for while the Rosemanowes site was solid granite, the Los Alamos site carried a relatively soft overlying volcanic material to a depth of 750 metres.

By the mid 1980s work of an experimental nature was in full swing at Rosemanowes, generating employment for almost 30 full-time personnel in the experimental field and a similar number in administration.

Dr Batchelor remained as project director for 13 years. Eventually he left the Geothermal Energy Project to take up a similar post with GeoScience. This was the end of Phase 2B. Dr Batchelor's place was taken in October 1986 by Mr Roger Parker from the Camborne School of Mines. He remained as Project Director until his retirement at the end of September 1991. Dr A.S.P. Green became the new director for the ensuing three months after which the Geothermal Project became the Camborne School of Mines Associates Limited (CSMA Ltd.). Set up in 1987, with Mr Parker as Managing Director in 1991, CSMA Ltd. had its origins at the School of Mines itself. Mr Parker relinquished both posts upon his retirement.

Above: *Aerial view of the site.*
Below, right: *Steam issuing from the wellhead.*

The next Managing Director of CSMA Ltd at Rosemanowes was Mr Brian Calver. He took up his position on 1 October 1991 and relinquished it on 31 March 1992, when Dr A.S.P. Green again became the Managing Director of a company which literally had become a consultancy company in demand the world over for its expertise in the exploration of geothermal energy, mining, oil and gas, as well as renewable energy.

Dr M.J. Ripley became the new Chief Executive Officer of CSMA Ltd on 1 May 1998, retaining this position until 18 June 1999, when the company was sold again – to ABB.

At the time of going to press there are 18 full-time members of staff as well as two part-time members plus a part-time caretaker/cleaner and one temporary receptionist.

On 19 July 1999, the new company, ABB, issued a press release setting out its aims:

ABB is a globalised technology and engineering company serving customers in power transmission and distribution; automation; oil and gas and petrochemicals; industrial products and contracting; as well as financial services.

The ABB Group currently employs about 160 000 people in more than 100 countries.

Chapter 12: Kennall Vale

The years teach much which the days never know.

Ralph Waldo Emerson 1803-82

The Kennall Valley has been the scene of great industry, of toil, tragedy and supreme tranquillity. It is in the latter capacity that this exquisitely beautiful part of the parish will continue into the foreseeable future with the recognition of its intrinsic qualities and timeless charm.

Stithians is not identified in the Domesday Book of 1086 but we can date the manor of Kennall to 1201 when the name appeared as Kennel. It is no surprise to discover that the name has become altered down the centuries; variants include Keniel in 1296, Kenel in 1278, 1309 and 1349, Kynel in 1302 and 1338, and Kenyel in 1376. By 1396 it had become Kennell. The spelling today, generally speaking, is Kennall.

J.E.L. Gover was of the view that the name may have come from an old stream which contained the element 'ial' meaning 'fertile upland'.

Dr John Kennall was the vicar of Wendron and Helston in 1536 and was recorded in Veysey's *Valor Ecclesiasticus* of the same year as Johannes Kenall. He read law and received his degree from Oxford in 1540 and a doctorate followed in 1553. In the inventory of the church goods at the time of the Reformation, John Kenall signed as vicar of Wendron and Helston. We learn that the Reverend John Kenall, LLD, was appointed vicar of Gwennap on 27 April 1550, Archdeacon of Oxford in 1561 and was Canon of Exeter at the time of his death in 1592.

The unusual surname leads one to ponder whether Dr John Kenall may have been a scion of a family with origins in the Kennall settlement. The distinguished historian, the late A.L. Rowse, CH, referred to Richard Carew's *Survey of Cornwall* (1602) in which the latter wrote of the Cornish language and the fact that 'the Lords Prayer, the Apostles Creed and the Ten Commandments have been much used in Cornish beyond all remembrance'. It was also said that 'the principal

The Paper Mill at Little Plymouth, c.1900.

The Paper Mill float for the 1897 jubilee, pictured outside Prince's House, Truro. The slogan reads: Kennal Mills make paper bags, Bags of Fibre, pulp and rags, One & all this jubilee, Should uphold home industry.

love and knowledge of this [the Cornish] language lived in Dr Kenall the Civilian and with him lieth buried'.

Water power on the Kennall River has probably been used since before 1659 when a dwelling was converted from a former blowing house which would have required a water wheel to power the bellows. In 1824 we are told that:

> On the south border of this manor is a fine stream of water called Kennall River. It rises in the parish of Wendron and in running on to Kennall turns a number of grist mills, and a hammer mill. At Kennall it works an extensive paper manufactory. Farther on in Kennall Wood it turns six water wheels, some very large, and works an hydraulic machine for manufacturing gunpowder. To work this machinery the river falls 84 feet perpendicularly, and it is constantly turning runners upwards of 22 tons weight on gunpowder. The river afterwards passes on to Ponsanooth where it turns a number of grist mills, three fulling mills, spinning jennies, carding machines, and works a large paper manufactory. At Wheal Magdelen Mine it works a large water engine and mill; and at Perran Wharf, where it falls into the tide, it turns two grist mills, a machine for lifting water, a saw mill, a large hammer mill, a boring mill and some turning lathes.
>
> This river from its source to its union with the sea runs about five miles and a half in which short distance it turns thirty nine water wheels all in active and full employ. It may be doubted if within the same short distance another such stream can be found in England.

Stithians parishioners have found employment in many Kennall Vale industries. William Tucker, who was resident at Kennall Vale House in 1840, was involved in the paper-making industry and established the manufactory at Little Plymouth.

The business was in existence in 1809 and aimed to produce writing papers of superior quality. Advertisements offered a variety of paper: blotting, blue and cartridge, thick and thin post, plain, black and gilt edge, and white and brown in all sizes. The mill passed into new hands by 1851 when Messrs W.S. Williams and W.S. Powning were producing paper and millboard.

Towards the end of the 19th century old calico and hessian flour bags were amongst the materials used in the paper-making process and these were obtained from mills in Plymouth. A paper-making machine 54 inches wide was installed in 1885 extending the mill's capacity.

By the 1890s there were six employees from Stithians engaged in the paper mill. Four were paper makers, John Knuckey (46), Lavinia Opie (46), Mary Collins (25) and Selina Spargo (24). John Knuckey's daughters, Elizabeth (16) and Mary (13), worked as paper finishers, and the paper sorter was Angelina Dunstan (14). The mill ceased production a few years later.

Farming was an extremely important aspect of life at Kennall and the following announcement in the *Royal Cornwall Gazette* appeared on 30 October 1813:

> TO BE SOLD BY TENDER
> THE FEE IN POSSESSION OF THE SOUTHERN PART OF THE BARTON OF KENNALL
> IN THE PARISH OF STITHIANS IN THE COUNTY OF CORNWALL
>
> ... consisting of about 85 acres of good corn or grazing land; a dwelling house; a large barn with a threshing machine, 6-stall stable, and all other necessary outhouses; now and for 50 years past in the occupation of the Proprietor.
>
> The premises are situated adjoining the turnpike road about midway between Truro and Helston about 5 miles from Redruth, 4 from Penryn, 6 from Falmouth and 3½ from Perran-Wharf, where lime and sea sand may be procured. The Estate lies compact, level, near good markets and good roads, and is in such a high state of Cultivation that it needs no other recommendation.
>
> ALSO
>
> The reversion in Fee, after the death of one life aged 52, of and in all those well-watered
>
> FLOUR AND GRIST MILLS
> CALLED KENNALL MILLS
>
> ... with the Dwelling House, Stable, Garden, etc. and about 7 acres of very rich Meadow Land adjoining the above Premises now in the occupation of Mr E.M. Scott. The Mills are well adapted for any purpose where wheels of 20 feet in diameter, with a constant supply of water, are required.
>
> Tenders for either of the above Tenements, separately or for the both together, may be sent to the Proprietor William Bath, Esq., at Kennall until the last day of November next, soon after which the Person whose Tender is accepted will be informed thereof. Other Particulars may be known by applying to the said William Bath, or to Mr J. Haward, Land Surveyor, Truro; and Plans of the Premises may be seen at the King's Arms Inn, Bodmin, and the Angel Hotel, Helston.
>
> NB It is supposed that tin and copper lodes run through the Premises, 27 October 1813.

Top: *Kennall Bridge, 1970s. The building with a chimney and small-paned window was an office and a familiar sight for customers of Polkinhorn and Company, the millers and corn merchants. Several generations of Polkinhorns were connected with Kennall Vale until the late 1980s.* Above: *Some of the buildings of the mill complex, c.1900. The lower cottage has been restored in recent years. Mr John Bolitho is pictured in the left foreground, father of Frank Bolitho.*

A quarry was set up in the vale about 1910 and operated until the demise of the industry. The work areas and buildings of the granite quarry were on the site of the old gunpowder works for which Kennall Vale is noted.

The first gunpowder factory in the area was established in 1809 in Cosawes Wood by Messrs Nicholls and Gill at a time when gunpowder was being brought into the country to meet the demand of 4000 barrels (1 barrel = 80lbs) each year for mining and quarrying. The well-known Fox family secured licenses for the manufacture of gunpowder in 1811, which complemented their existing enterprises at the Perran Foundry and in mining and shipping (as well as certain business interests in Wales).

The location at Kennall Vale was considered ideal for the manufacture of explosives but to the detriment of Cosawes; by1844 the latter was also owned by the Fox family.

The business was successful and expansion followed. By 1875 the Kennall Gunpowder Company comprised a manager's house, the original works, a sulphur mill and associated premises, a saltpetre refinery, a charcoal mill in Ponsanooth, magazines and cottages. An important addition was the Roches Wood Works with improved equipment, and these premises were licensed for production in 1844.

Sadly and inevitably accidents occurred and reports appeared in the press. On 25 February 1825, for example, the following was printed in the *Royal Cornwall Gazette*:

A melancholy accident occurred in the powder mills near Ponsanooth on Friday last. About half-past twelve o'clock on that day, the mixing house, in which were four persons at their usual employment, was blown up. Two of the men escaped almost without injury but the woman, named Rutter, died on Friday night; the third man named Weeks, survived until Sunday morning. Although it is generally difficult to account for accidents in powder mills, the present was occasioned by the old woman who had been roasting potatoes at a considerable distance from the works, and had unconsciously carried a spark of fire on her clothes to the mill. This was seen almost immediately on her entrance but before it could be prevented it fell and the explosion instantly followed.

The Bickford Smith Works below Kennall Vale.

And on 17 June 1826 the same paper revealed:

Another of those melancholy accidents which so frequently happen in powder manufactories occurred at Kennall Vale powder mill on Saturday last. The particulars of this unfortunate occurrence... that two men named Henry Martin and James Weeks were killed and another man severely hurt by the explosion. On the cause of the accident we are not distinctly informed, but understand that the mill itself has not sustained much damage.

A further explosion was recorded in December 1828 and on this occasion no one was injured, but in May 1838 the *West Briton* reported that five mills blew up in succession and that part of a roof was found a mile from the premises. Understandably the event caused great alarm in the locality and on this occasion one man was seriously injured. In January 1841 John Martin was killed, leaving a widow and two children. He was buried in the churchyard at Stithians and the vicar's sermon was so highly regarded that it was later produced in printed form. Kennall House, the residence of the manager of the works, Richard Lanyon, 'suffered considerably. Several windows were broken and some of the furniture injured'. In 1843 three mills blew up, but a tragedy in November 1887 resulted in an investigation by HM Inspector of Explosives for the Secretary of State for the Home Department, who recorded that:

... one man, William Dunstan, was known to be at work within the building at the time of the explosion and another, James Paddy, was engaged with a horse and cart taking powder to and from the building.

William Dunstan (42), father of a large family, was killed and parts of his body flung five yards and thirty yards away. James Paddy (50-60 years) was found lying in a watercourse about 15 yards away having suffered burns to the face and hands, a broken arm and leg as well as head injuries. Conscious, the poor man was able to tell what he thought had happened; he died in the Royal Cornwall Infirmary at Truro, having given a clear account of events to the Inspector who came to the conclusion that the accident may have

The picturesque setting of Kennall Mill.

arisen from fire being caused by William Dunstan at the boxes (that is, unpressed powder and also that removed from the press); in the press itself; or by a spark from the watch-house chimney, which he felt was improbable. The Coroner's jury returned a verdict of accidental deaths and exonerated the company from blame, with which HM Inspector was in agreement.

In 1889 the company employed 50 people. By 1891 only seven men from Stithians were working there, including: Edwin Lidgey (Manager), 49-year-old storekeeper Peter Chegwidden and 45-year-old Mark John (both from Tregost, and the latter the foreman millwright who gave evidence in 1887 to HM Inspector investigating the double tragedy). The others were: 51-year-old Edward Martin (from Tregolls), William Spargo (45, from Trewithen), Thomas Opie (59, of East Road) and Samuel Martin (29, from Tretheague) – all four of these men gunpowder makers. By 1893 the workforce had dwindled to 20 and this decline continued until 1898 when the company was sold for £25 826.17s.6d. to Messrs Curtis and Harvey. After 1870 high explosives (including dynamite) had arrived, and doubtless this spurred the company to sell before the value fell even more.

The saltpetre refinery remained unused until the 1920s when Messrs Bickford, Smith & Co, (manufacturers of 'The Patent Safety Rod' – later the 'Safety Fuze') set up a factory for the manufacture of a specialised product – Kennall Gutta Percha, used as waterproofing to cover safety-fuses.

Kennall Vale

Output of Gunpowder and Price per Ton Blasting Powder 1876-96

Year	Tons	Price
1876	436	£29.3s.10d.
1877	528½	28.1.3.
1878	500	29.13.8.
1879	446	28.15.4.
1880	335½	32.11.5.
1881	535½	29.13.11.
1882	449	29.19.0.
1883	400	32.6.0.
1884	257	35.18.11.
1885	233	30.1.5.
1886	119	34.7.0.
1887	161.	29.9.6.
1888	193	26.6.2.
1889	214	25.13.4.
1890	188	25.11.9.
1891	153.	29.7.0.
1892	146	28.18.4
1893	131	31.0.5
1894	137	28.2.1.
1895	90½	32.19.2
1896	78½	34.11.1

Gunpowder Sales to Fuse Factories, 1892:

Bickford, Smith & Co.	41 900 lbs
W. Bennetts, Son & Co.	30 000
British & Foreign	14 000
Unity Wood	13 150
W. Brunton	9100
E. Tangye	8650

In 1985 a new opportunity arose. Through the benevolence and understanding of Mr Ross Williams, owner of Kennall Vale, about 21 acres were leased on a long-term basis to the Cornwall Trust for Nature Conservation with the intention of managing the site as a reserve. The undertaking includes the conservation of the woodland, footpaths and trackways as well as the remains of Kennall's remarkable industrial site.

The Ponsanooth-born naturalist, Frederick Hamilton Davey, FLS (1868-1915), was dedicated to Kennall Vale where his fascination with birds and woodland flowers found inspiration. He worked for the Gunpowder Company as a road labourer when only 11 years old and subsequently as a book-keeper; the daily contact with wildlife added to his curiosity about Kennall Vale and his biography tells us that he found 'Wood Millet, Smooth Sedge and Tunbridge Filmy-Fern'. He produced a paper on the micro-organisms of Kennall and was awarded a second-class medal by the Royal Cornwall Polytechnic in 1892 and a subsequent contribution on the distribution of plants in the valley was printed by the Royal Institution of Cornwall. The current conservation plans would have fulfilled his most fervent wish.

In 1986 John R. Smith compiled 'The Kennall Vale Archaeological Report for the Cornwall Trust for Nature Conservation'. We will conclude with his words, surely a tribute to both industrial past and natural beauty:

The Kennall Gunpowder Company was remarkable amongst other Cornish powder makers in its degree of organisation and the extensive nature of its works. Initially set up to serve local needs, by 1870 its influence had spread beyond the County and its products were exported not only to the rest of Britain but overseas. In this respect, it can rightly be compared to the great symbols of Cornish Industry in the same period, the foundries such as Harvey's of Hayle. Like them, Kennall too withered and died in the face of the collapse of Cornish mining, the base upon which its prosperity depended.

Despite its wide ranging business connection the Kennall Company was typical of the time in its being essentially a local concern relating to and serving the needs of the community in which it stood. The technology required to operate the factory was readily comprehensible by the local workforce, and in essence represents an eighteenth century concept of manufacture, based upon the principles long established by corn millers and millwrights.

Disturbed at times by the inevitable accident, powder making was essentially a quiet, contemplative process, suited to men of a steady and reliable nature. A factor which especially endears Kennall Vale to modern hearts was its ability to co-exist in harmony with the valley in which it stood; all accounts stress the beauty of the site, in itself partly a creation of the powder makers as they planted trees to screen the buildings.

The lasting impressions of Kennall Vale are of the factory at night, waterwheels rumbling in the darkness, with buildings seen dimly lit by a chain of lanterns hanging in the trees; or on a summer's day with the leats sparkling through the woods and the horse and cart plodding up the valley. Kennall Vale exists as a monument to those men and the values of another age.

Those of us who remember with affection childhood excursions on summer picnics, collecting wild flowers and the sight of a kingfisher will rejoice at Kennall's new role.

Right: *The substantial and grand Kennall Bridge, 1970s.*

Memorandum of an Agreement Made This... Day of November 1783 Between Michael Nowell of the Town of Falmouth in Cornwall of the One Part and Thomas Reed of Trevalis in the Said County of the Other Part.

As Follows

The said Michael Nowell Hath Let and the said Thomas Reed hath taken All that the said Michael Nowell's Ten Twelfths or Ten parts in Twelve in a certain Lode running in and through the Tenement of Penhalurick in the Parish of Stithyans and One hundred fathoms to the north and the same to the south of the said Lode which said Lode is supposed to be Tresavean Lode and also all that the entire Lode in Trelusback with one hundred fathoms each side of the said Lode.

Conditions

1. That the Term be for twenty one years from 25 December 1783.

2. That one tenth part [of] the whole in eight parts [is] to be divided of all tyn, copper, ore, and other mettals and minerals to be laid out in the usual manner for the said Michael Novell which shall be rose or gotten in the said Tenement of Trelusback.

3. That $^{10}/_{12}$th or ten parts of twelve parts of one eighth (amended to one tenth) of all copper ore and other mettals (Except Tin) be laid out in the usual manner to and for the said Michael Nowell which shall be gotten or raised in the said Tenement of Penhalurick.

4. That the said Mine be immediately begun and carried on all working time and be wrought effectually with six able workmen at the least in the Addit end.

5. That all the shafts, addits and drifts be bound and kept open in a workmanlike manner and at the end of the said term to be delivered up in such good order.

6. Its mutualy agreed that were any part of the said premises of Penhalurick have Lawfull Tin Bounds, the Dues thereof shall be paid and laid out by one fourteenth to the Lords.

7. And it is also mutually agreed that One tenth dues of copper shall be paid instead of One Eighth untill the whole costs of bringing in the Addit and Working the same shall be fully paid and satisfied.

8. That no addit or drift shall be drove within three fathoms of the extent of the set hereby granted.

Lastly That sets and counterparts shall be forthwith prepared by Mr Nowell's Attorney at the Expense of the Taker.

(Royal Institution of Cornwall
Sett for Tin/Copper Nowell to Reed
U/14/21)

Chapter 13: Mining

Mining has played an important part in the lives of our ancestors but, as far as can be established, no substantial mining venture took place in the parish – no counting houses, engine houses, or associated artefacts have been discovered.

There were, however, extensive workings on the Wendron and Gwennap boundaries and Stithians was heavily dependent upon the mines for employment: a list of miners and tinners in 1798 reveals that 148 males (15-60-year-olds) earned their living in the industry. (The spaces in the list do not indicate unnamed candidates, but the entry of an address instead.).

TO THE CONSTABLE OF THE PARISH OF STITHIANS

To wit By Virtue of an Order from Sir John Morshead, Baronet, Lord Warden of the Stannaries in and for the said County, unto me directed, you are hereby required to make out a fair and true List, in writing, of all the Miners and Working Tinners usually, and at this Time dwelling within your Constablewick, between the Ages of Fifteen and Sixty Years, distinguishing therein which of them are willing to engage themselves to be armed, arrayed, trained and exercised, for the Defence of the Realm, and which of them are willing to engage, in Cases of Emergency, either gratuitously, or for Hire, and Pioneers or Labourers, and such of them as by Reason of Infirmity are incapable of active Service, according to the Form hereunto annexed; which List, 80 fairly made as aforesaid, you are hereby required to return to John Thomas Esq. Vicewarden of the Stannaries aforesaid at the house of John Blights the Sign of the Red Lion in Truro on saturday the twenty eighth day of April Instant by Ten O'Clock in the forenoon.

Given under my Hand this twenty third Day of April in the Year of our Lord 1798

William Spargo, High Constable

(Royal Institution of Cornwall; The Nalder Collection, Leases N/71)

	A LIST OF MINERS & TINNERS OF STYTHIANS BETWEEN THE AGES OF 15 AND 60 YEARS, 23 APRIL 1798			
1	Thos. Oppy	Ennis	55	Infirm
2	Thos. Oppy Junr	"	27	
3	Jas. Oppy Junr	"	16	
4	Francis Oppy	"	25	
5	Thos. Oppy	"	18	
6	Jas. Oppy	"	40	
7	Jas. Thomas	"	18	
8	Richard Reed	Crella	40	
9	Robt. Reed	"	38	
10	Dins. Reed	"	32	
11	Jno. Andrew	"	30	
12	Robt. Murtin	"	38	
13	Willm. Wicks	"	56	
14	Thos. Wicks	"	26	
15	Jno. Vencent	"	28	
16	Willm. Andrew	Tremol	30	
17	Walter Andrew	"	27	
18	Josh. Andrew	"	24	
19	Jas. Tozzer	Velandrucke	58	
20	Robt. Tozzer	"	19	
21	Jno. Knuckey	"	26	
22	Saml. Peters	Tregoning	55	Infirm
23	Saml. Peters	"	18	
24	Jno. Spargo	"	40	
25	Thos. Spargo	"	18	
26	Heny. Spargo	"	15	
27	Bent. Oppy	"	24	
28	Richd. Oppy	"	18	
29	Thos. Oppy	Tregoning	16	
30	Willm. Andrew	"	21	
31	Bent. Andrew	"	18	

32	Josh. Andrew	"	36
33	Nichs. Andrew	"	20
34	Willm. Andrew	"	18
35	Jas. Chegwyden	Tremenhear	34
36	Willm. Peters	"	30
37	Thos. Treloar	"	34
38	Nichs. Peters	Tory	38
39	Saml. Peters	"	28
40	Sampn. Peters	"	24
41	Thos. Peters	Gunvean	21
42	Heny. Peters	"	17
43	Thos. Peters	Trevales	40
44	Edwd. Martin	"	22
45	Geoe. Vencent	"	33
46	Heny. Crougy	"	24
47	Heny. Martin	Trewinsh	50
48	Jas. Martin	"	40
49	Jas. Wicks, Junr	"	30
50	Jas. Wicks	"	36
51	Hugh Wicks	"	16
52	Thos. Martin	"	28
53	Martin Martin	"	26
54	Jos. Martin	"	22
55	Jno. Murten, Senr	"	58
56	Jno. Murten, Junr	Trewinsh	28
57	Thos. Spargo	"	38
58	Jas. Spargo	"	20
59	Geoe. Murten	"	50
60	Peter Murten	"	22
61	George Murten, Junr	"	19
62	Heny. Bishop	Gribbis	38
63	Jas. Knuckey	"	20
64	Jas. Knuckey, Junr	"	18
65	Hugh Knuckey	"	26
66	Jas. Peters	Tregost	24
67	Jas. Spargo	"	26
68	Phillip Rickerd	"	23
69	Jno. Andrew	"	26
70	Jas. Andrew	"	27
71	Jno. Oppy	Wood	21
72	Jas. Oppy	"	19
73	Jno. Oppy	Trebarva	24
74	Saml. Collins	"	32
75	Willm. Collins	Trebost	21
76	Jas. Collins	"	18
77	Nichs. Spargo	"	26
78	Edwd. Spargo	"	40
79	Stepn. Spargo	"	21
80	Saml. Spargo	"	18
81	Hugh Phillips	Custpost	52
82	Hugh Phillips, Junr	"	17
83	Bent. Odger	Burncoose	59
84	Jno. Odger	"	24
85	Dins. Reed	"	32
86	Richd. Collins	"	24
87	Jas. Collins	"	22
88	Willm. Murtin	"	34
89	Jno. Sarah	Tregols	31
90	Nichs. Andrew	"	24
91	Jno. Andrews	"	22
92	Willm. Martin	"	30

93	Wm. Wicks	Tresenwith	26
94	Hugh Knucky	Carn	32
95	Collan Dunstan	"	24
96	Willm. Andrew	"	28
97	Peter Andrew	"	24
98	Heny. Dunstan	"	22
99	Mathw. Hill	Penmenar	21
100	Jas. Odger	"	20
101	Wm. Dunstan	Gunlaze	38
102	Jno. Dunstan	"	46
103	Jno. Dunstan	"	22
104	Thos. Dunstan	"	20
105	Thos. Treloar	"	44
106	Wm. Bath	"	56
107	Jno. Kemp	"	52
108	Tresm. Bath	"	32
109	---		
110	Richd. Oppy	Curvollick	56
111	Wm. Oppy	"	27
112	Wm. Hicks	"	38
113	Wm. Martin	"	32
114	Wm. Dunstan	"	58
115	Wm. Dunstan	"	20
116	Jno. Dunstan	Curvollick	18
117	Wm. Peard	"	28
118	(John ?) Reed	"	22
119	Jos. Reed	"	20
120	? (Buzza or Tozzer)	"	--
121	Thos. Odger	"	57
122	Jno. Odger	"	22
123	Jno. Odger, Senr	"	27
124	Bent. Odger	"	21
125	--		
126	Jno. Oppy	Carnsidga	47
127	Jno. Oppy, Junr	"	21
128	Thos. Oppy	"	19
129	Richd. Oppy	"	17
130	Bent. Odger	"	28
131	Jos. Odger	Trenbroth	22
132	Jacob Odger	"	19
133	Jerh. Odger	"	17
134	Thos. Spargo	"	45
135	Nichs. Odger	"	38
136	Thos. Odger	"	18
137	Jno. Wicks	"	37
138	--		
139	Wm. Phillips	Treskewis	27
140	Willm. Spargo	"	18
141	--		
142	Bent. Knuckey	Trelvias	27
143	Heny. Martin	Trewence	32
144	Jas. Knuckey	Hendra	32
145	Jas. Bath	Menerdew	24
146	Stepn. Bailey	"	18
147	--		
148	Jno. Dunstan	Penhalvear	28
149	Bent. Odger	"	27
150	Jno. Odger	"	24
151	Nichs. Odger	"	20
152	Heny. Welmet	Nanpean	38
153	Richd. Welmet	"	26

Carnvullock Farmhouse with Reg Toy, the farmer, in the entrance. Carnvullock had a fine granite front and was one of the many houses which were bulldozed and flattened in preparation for the flooding of the valley.

The very last of Little Ambella, one of the ill-fated properties, 3 January 1953.

Chapter 14: Stithians Reservoir

Kerrier Rural District Council first considered the present site of the Stithians reservoir on the Kennall River in 1945 when making proposals to improve supplies of water in its district. The Joint Committee was formed in 1956 to include members of Camborne-Redruth UDC (Urban District Council), and Truro UDC. At its head as Chairman was Councillor Admiral E.L.S. King, CB, MVO, DEL (Kerrier Rural District Council).

A public enquiry followed in 1960, work commenced on the site in 1962 and impounding in 1965. The treatment works was completed in 1967. The following year, 1968, the South West Water Board was formed with Stithians as its major source. Almost immediately a need arose to increase the yield of 2.7mgd (millions of gallons per day) to 4.9mgd. This was achieved by embarking upon the Kennall Vale scheme which augmented the yield by pumping water from two miles further downstream. All of this, of necessity, wrought great changes for the local folk concerned who were farming the land or who had their homes in the area of the valleys which were designated to be flooded. Their homes, their way of life, all was gone for ever. Some of the farmers moved to farms elsewhere, some found retirement as an alternative, others were offered compensation, and some, who had only part of their farms taken from them, carried on with a reduced acreage. Others were offered the residue of land from farms which happened to be surplus to requirement for the creation of the reservoir.

For the men who plan and mastermind such schemes, a reservoir is just another project, but to the folk who live and farm the land in the valleys concerned it is probably just about the biggest upheaval in their lives, and the Stithians scheme was to prove no exception. Almost 20 farmsteads were engulfed as well as several cottages and acres and acres of good farmland, not forgetting several tracts of waste and croft land.

A uniquely-designed arch dam was planned on an area of kaolinised granite – granite which, over time, has become decomposed. Few such designs are to be found in the UK but most of the others are in Scotland, it being a particular design more commonly found in the ravine areas of Europe.

By 1963 virtually all the valley folk had gone, their homes and farm buildings reduced to rubble. New roads had to be made to divert those which had previously entered the lake area of the proposed reservoir, the surface of which would total 270 acres. The reservoir itself was to have a storage capacity of over one billion gallons of water. In its deepest part it would be 62 feet, and a total

Once the home of Mr J. Kemp, East Menorlue Farmhouse is now buried deep under the water.

The Working Reservoir

Above: *The completed treatment works viewed from the top of the dam with the staff homes in the background.*

Above: *The reservoir pumping station, photographed c.1967 (the time of opening).*
Above right*: The dam, September 1964. The small child, who can just be made out standing beside it, shows the massive height of the structure. The photograph was taken shortly before the flow of water from the Kennall River was interrupted to fill the reservoir. A certain gallonage had to be allowed to run freely and uninterrupted so as to allow farmers and others an adequate supply for cattle, etc.*

Little Ambella

Left: *Little Ambella in its heyday and (bottom) a sketch of the farmhouse by Helen Dunstan.*

Below: *In 1976 the summer's severe drought reduced the water to such a degree that the former field hedges were revealed. In this photograph the road to the farms at Ambella and East Menorlue is clearly visible. Many such roads, once revealed, could be seen to have their gateposts and metal fastenings still intact.*

Below: *A gaunt and bare stump of a gorse bush and granite debris from the one-time farmhouse creates a sombre reminder of earlier times.*

Left: *Allan Smith sitting on Carnvullock Bridge during a visit to his aunt, Mrs L. Corey, and her family at Carncrees Farm, c.1930. The bridge was later swamped by the reservoir.*
Right: *Alison Corey and her niece, Anne Corey, looking for trout in the Kennall River. It was the height of summer, 1951, and Carnvullock Bridge was almost hidden by foxgloves and tall grasses.*

An exposed tree stump looks forlornly over an equally dismal reservoir during the drought of the late 1980s.

STITHIANS RESERVOIR

The dam, nearing completion, viewed from downstream.

of 22 000 acres of gathering ground brought into use. The finished perimeter fence would measure 11 000 yards in circumference.

On Friday 13 October 1967 a commissioning ceremony of both dam and treatment works took place. The pumping station and the treatment works, downstream of the dam itself, catered for a flow of 120 000 gallons of water per hour. A reinforced concrete reservoir, with a one-million-gallon capacity, was built on the top of Carnmenellis Hill supplying the higher levels of Kerrier RDC and Camborne/Redruth UDC.

Three staff bungalows were built at the entrance to the site adjacent to the fairly large car-parking area. A fourth bungalow was added at a later date; however, they have all since been sold to individuals as the treatment works has been automated and staff members no longer reside on site.

The reservoir attracts many visitors on a daily basis, often from beyond our own shores. It is also a popular area for fishing, sailing and wind surfing. The drought during the summer of 1976 brought the water to an all-time low and revealed much of the rubble produced by levelling houses and outbuildings. However, the farm lanes, complete with hedges and gateposts, still with their gate hangings, appeared once more, and virtually intact – a sight which must have stirred many memories.

Water from the clear tank is now pumped into three reservoirs – Carnmenellis, Lanner Hill (supplying Redruth) and the third at Roskrow Wood (supplying the Lizard Peninsula). Water gravitates to a fourth zone covering a part of the Carrick District Council from Perran-ar-Worthal in the south to St Agnes in the north.

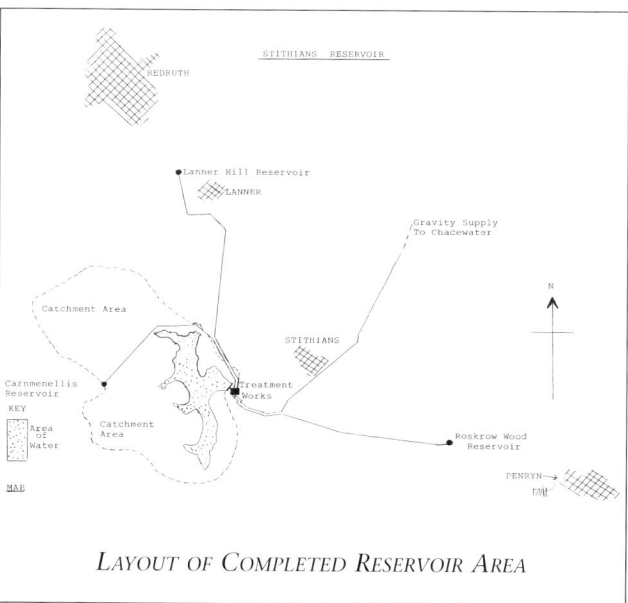

LAYOUT OF COMPLETED RESERVOIR AREA

Tregonning Mill with members of the family of Hannibal Johns standing in front of the buildings.

Bennet (Ben) Andrew Martin and his wife, Lilla May Martin, pictured in front of their farmhouse at Carn Meor. With Mr and Mrs Martin is Gwen Braybrooke, their wartime evacuee (having returned from her London home some time after the war for a visit). Ben Martin had spent almost all of his life as a farmer/pig dealer.

Chapter 15: Some of the Many Renowned Stithians Folk

THE ODGERS BROTHERS – 'THE WISE MEN OF STITHIANS'

Although there are no photographs of these remarkable men to speak of, they were undoubtedly exceptional and must surely find a place here. They were the brothers Nicholas Odgers and Jacob Odgers, BA. They were totally unassuming, non materialistic, self-made men, clever, and in their thinking and reasoning they were a century ahead of their time.

Nicholas became a schoolmaster and his brother a teacher in a somewhat lesser capacity. Nicholas wrote several books and later he was to establish the *Redruth Independent Newspaper*, also becoming its editor. Both men were Methodists and local preachers.

In June 1947, more than 100 years after the brothers were born, a local newspaper printed a lengthy article eulogising both men. The piece was entitled, 'The Wise Men of Stithians' and appeared in the *Falmouth Packet*.

The stationer's shop in Penryn Street, Redruth, run by Nicholas Odgers. In the photograph are Mrs Minnie Martin and Mrs Jane Odgers, daughter and wife, respectively, of Nicholas. Also in the picture is Mr Charles Martin, Nicholas' son-in-law. Mrs Odgers was formerly Miss Jane Knuckey, a member of an old and respected Stithians family, and a first cousin of Miss Jane Hellings.

Lizzie Sherdy (1820-1905/6), whose real name was Elizabeth Dunstan, was born at Crag Brawse, a little hamlet near Chacewater, and lived in various parishes in the Truro and Redruth area with her husband Jimmy. She had a small cottage and sweet shop in Stithians at one stage and would walk for miles with her husband to Flora Day, feasts and tea treats to sell her wares. One night Jimmy went about smashing the china in their house and, as punishment, Lizzie made him a pasty containing some of the remnants of their tableware! Hence the name Lizzie Sherdy.

SOME OF THE MANY RENOWNED STITHIANS FOLK

THE PIONEERING KNUCKEY BROTHERS

Born in Stithians, the pioneering Knuckey brothers attended Stithians School before emigrating to Australia with their parents and siblings in 1848. Richard Randall Knuckey (*above*) was born on 23 October 1842 and his brother, John, was born on 29 March 1845. They were the sons of Richard and Persis Knuckey (née Reed). Richard figured largely in the Overland Telegraph Cable Line Project across Australia from Adelaide in the South, to Darwin in the north, a distance of some 2000 miles. He was especially prominent in that he was a man possessed of a profound ability as a surveyor and proved himself to be outstanding in his field. He had been appointed as a Senior Surveyor in 1868 under George Goyder, Surveyor General of the South Australian Survey Department.

A main street in Darwin is named Knuckey Street after him, in honour of the part he played in the major survey of the town (formerly known as Palmerston). He later surveyed vast tracts of the outback, traversing hitherto unexplored and highly dangerous territory, as well as areas in central Australia – all at great personal risk to himself. He undertook these adventures prior to the eventual link-up with Australia and England via the east through Java, Darwin and, eventually, Porthcurno in Cornwall (which provided the very first physical link between Cornwall and the rest of the world). There were, of course, other surveyors employed in the project, but Richard Randall Knuckey figured highly amongst their numbers. His was the name attributed by the Surveyor General and A.J. Mitchell (a surveyor who had worked alongside Knuckey) to the Knuckey Lagoon, ten miles east of Darwin, and near Stuart Highway. Richard was appointed the first Line Inspector in 1870 continuing after the line was joined in 1872.

John Randall Knuckey was to follow his brother as Line Inspector in 1874 and made a substantial contribution to the expansion of the telegraph line and its maintenance.

Right: *The heavy broken line denotes the 'central section' of the overland cable for the telegraph, the laying of which was overseen by surveyors including Richard Randall Knuckey.*

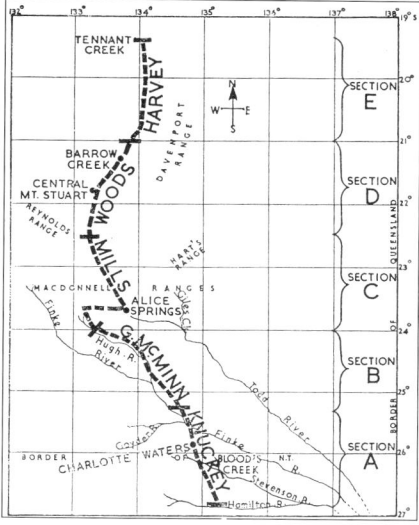

Richard Randall Knuckey (holding theodolite) and survey party with the Northern Territory Expedition, 1869.

Miss Hellings receiving her British Empire Medal from Lord Macintosh in London, 9 March 1954.

Group taken at an Area National Savings Conference at Camborne on 2 June 1954, with Miss Hellings receiving her 35 years' Service Bar, as a National Savings worker, from Mr T.F.E. Jakeman (Regional Representative). Inset: The British Empire Medal (centre) surrounded by all the badges of office which Miss Hellings was entitled to wear.

SOME OF THE MANY RENOWNED STITHIANS FOLK

MISS JANE HELLINGS, BEM (1882-1963).

Miss Jane (Janie) Hellings, BEM, was born at Ennis and Carbis, Crellow. She became Janie to all who knew her. She was a unique woman in that she had held most of the offices open to ladies in the parish, even being among the first of the lady presidents of the famed Stithians Agricultural Association (Mrs D.M. Briddon being the very first in 1954, and Miss Hellings the second in 1958). She was the first female churchwarden at the Parish Church and was for 40 years head of the Junior and Infant's School in Stithians.

Miss Hellings was Honorary Secretary of the newly-formed Stithians Women's Institute in January 1937 and in 1954 she still held that same position. The same year she was awarded the British Empire Medal for her outstanding achievements in collecting over £44 000 for National Savings since the formation of that association in 1917 and continuing through both wars and the inter-war period. In May 1946 Miss Hellings received a communication from the Lord Chamberlain stating that he had been 'Commanded by Their Majesties to invite Miss J. Hellings to an Afternoon Tea Party in the Garden of Buckingham Palace on Thursday 6th June 1946'. This was to be a party especially for representative workers in the National Savings Movement. These workers were selected by Local Savings Committees in the United Kingdom. It was, indeed, a proud moment for Janie Hellings, she was a truly remarkable person in that she gave untiringly of herself in whatsoever capacity she happened to be working – and these were myriad.

Left: *Janie on a windy day in Fore Street, Redruth, and* (right) *drawing water from the village pump*

THE HONOURABLE JAMES MARTIN, MLC

Born at Foundry, Stithians, in 1821 into a family which owned and ran Bryant's Foundry making shovels for farmers and miners, James helped in the foundry during his early years, later training as a millwright before going to work at Tresavean, a Gwennap copper mine. In order to gain further experience he eventually emigrated (in 1847) to Southern Australia, arriving in Adelaide on 7 July 1847.

Then aged 27, he married Christina Fox, a fellow passenger on the same boat from Plymouth as that on which he himself had travelled. Shortly afterwards James and his new wife left Adelaide and moved to Gawler, seeing possibilities there for manufacturing farm machinery as large tracts of land were being taken over by farmers and new mining ventures were being considered. The couple left the city on a dray with just James' furniture and a few tools. His immediate task on arrival in Gawler, then a bush hamlet, was to fell a tree and to make workbenches and a lathe.

James had perceived early on in Gawler that, owing to the huge ore-carrying traffic through the town from the copper mines in the north, here was a magnificent opportunity, and one not to be missed. He was quick to take advantage and to start manufacturing bullock-drawn wagons, and in a very short time was employing 30 men in a factory which eventually produced 15 000 reaping machines as well as other kinds of farm machinery. He also branched out to manufacture equipment for miners, as well as bridges and, finally, locomotives.

In April 1890 the State's very first locally-built locomotive steamed down Gawler's main street pulling four crowded carriages. The Governor himself was at the controls and Gawler turned out en-masse to cheer them on their way. Four years later, in December 1894, the Foundry of James Martin and Company had produced its one hundredth locomotive. James had continued to produce farm machinery, including ploughs, scarifiers, chaff cutters, reaping machines, etc.

Later in life James is reported to have said, 'For the first little while I was here it was a terrible job to get along – sometimes after paying my men only a portion of their wages, I had not 4d. left to take a letter out of the Post Office'. Then came the Gold Rush of 1851 to the Victoria gold fields. James joined those who went there but soon returned home.

James Martin was held in great esteem in Gawler, indeed he is remembered as 'The Father of Gawler', having spent his life there and doing great public service to the town. He was elected Alderman in 1857, becoming Mayor in 1860 and he was one of the founder members of Gawler Institute (becoming its President in 1861). He was Worshipful Master of the Freemason's Lodge, Director of the Building Society and a Captain of the Gawler Rifles after starting out as a Private. He was a member of the Council of the Gawler School of Mines and a member for Barossa in the House of Assembly for eight years until March 1868, as well as a Member of the Legislative Council for 14 years (a high honour). James Martin did much to bring Gawler into the 20th century and will always be remembered with affection there.

The James Martin engineering empire has virtually disappeared now; all that remains today of a factory which covered 18 acres and employed 700 men is the great archway and wall in Calton Street to mark the site of Martin's Phoenix Foundry. James died in December 1899. The cortège was a mile long and the funeral service had ended before the rear of the cortège had even reached the gates of the cemetery of Willaston! In 1903 a statue was erected in his memory. A locomotive, No. 245 to have been manufactured, stands as a memorial in Gawler's Parklands.

Above: The Honourable James Martin
Below: The marble memorial in St Stythians Church, dedicated to the memory of James Martin and family.

SOME OF THE MANY RENOWNED STITHIANS FOLK

Gawler's first locally-built locomotive, which was driven through the main street by the Governor of the State pulling four crowded carriages.

BOB DINGLE – ANTARCTIC EXPLORER

A meteorologist, Bob Dingle, born in Stithians, was awarded the Polar Medal in 1954 for his work in establishing Australia's Antarctic base. Son of Mr and Mrs William Dingle, Bob was educated at Helston and in recognition of his work two Antarctic features were named after him. They are Dingle's Dome and Dingle Lake. Pioneering from Melbourne, Bob Dingle eventually sailed on the *Magga Dan* on 5 January 1959, with some 14 men in his charge. This was his fifth Antarctic trip.

The Australian Minister of External Affairs commended Bob's work in Antarctica and added that there was no one more suitable to be officer-in-charge.

Above, inset: *W.J.R. (Bob) Dingle.*
Main picture: *Bob's mother, Mrs Miriam Jane Dingle (on the right), at home with her parents, Catharine Spargo Reed and Robert James Kemp Reed, at Albany Villa, Crellow Hill, c.1930s.*

107

Mrs Louie Veall Ford

Mrs Louie Veall Ford of Crellow Vean, Stithians – seen here perusing her congratulatory telegram from HM Queen Elizabeth II on reaching her 100th birthday on 16 May 1996. Her sister, Mrs Alberta Williams of Plymouth, can be seen doing the same thing in the picture on the wall behind her. She, too, had reached 100 (and beyond to 103!). Mrs Ford, a widow for the past 21 years (her husband Anthony died in December 1978), celebrated her 103rd birthday in May of 1999, a remarkable feat indeed. No one in Stithians has ever before attained that great age but she is still very alert and positive in her outlook and when she survives into the year 2000 she will have lived in three centuries! Both Mrs Ford and her sister, Mrs Williams, were born in Stithians, daughters of Mr Thomas Opie, a local preacher, trustee, Sunday-School officer and a staunch Liberal, as well as Clerk to the Parish Council from December 1894 until his demise in 1937, a period of just over 42 years.

Right: *Mrs Louie Veall Ford, on her 100th birthday, looking justifiably proud of herself, and reading her congratulatory telegram from the Queen.*

Major Jack Rodda Williams

Major Jack Rodda Williams was appointed headmaster to Stithians County Primary School in 1948, a post he was to retain for 26 years until his retirement. His interests were many and varied. After retiring from teaching, Jack R. (as he was known to almost everyone in the parish), took a post in the finance department at County Hall, Truro, and, as well as that, became a part-time accountant at the Cross-roads Motel at Scorrier, near Redruth. He was involved in many aspects of Stithians life. He was the Honorary General Secretary of the Stithians Agricultural Association for 20 years, following which he became Honorary Treasurer of that association for the next 12 years. During that time Jack organised both an Annual Dinner Dance for the association and, for many years, trips to various venues in Europe.

Major Williams completed 50 years as Parish Councillor, 11 of which were as Chairman of the Council. He was a founder member of the Arthritis and Rheumatism Council, a member of the British Legion and, for over 30 years, a trustee of the Penmennor Methodist Church.

Jack Williams was always ready to help local organisations and must have audited the accounts for almost every single one. This he did with a willingness beyond compare and all on a voluntary basis in his own leisure time. He did much for the improvement of the parish of Stithians, working unceasingly and untiringly. He died in March 1999 and his life in Stithians will long be remembered.

JOHN SPARGO (1876-1966)

Born at Longdowns, Stithians, in 1876, and just inside the parish boundary, John Spargo commenced work at the age of ten as a tinner in a nearby mine. He knew the meaning of poverty whilst growing up and vowed to improve his lot in later life. He married Prudence Edwards whilst working as a stonecutter in Cardiff in 1901. However, having been offered a rare opportunity of owning a newsagency and tobacconists cum confectionery shop on Lower East Side, New York, the Spargos left Cardiff to take up the offer – it seemed they had nothing to lose.

Upon their arrival in that city they found that John's stepfather, who had made the offer, had died. The promised shop did not materialise, so John secured a position with work on a Jewish encyclopaedia, later becoming the author of numerous accomplished newspaper articles and even a number of books.

John's wife died three years after their arrival in New York, leaving him with an infant son. He remarried in 1905 but the child died in infancy and, residing by that time in Vermont, New England (where he was to spend the rest of his life), John became Chairman of the Socialist Party after two years, as well as a member of the National Executive Committee.

Having studied the history of the Russian Revolution in depth, John Spargo became advisor to President Woodrow Wilson on Russian affairs in 1919. During the ensuing eight years he found himself engrossed in politics. From 1927 to 1954 Spargo was heavily involved in the founding of the Bennington Museum of which he became a director as well as curator until his retirement in 1954 from the post of Director-Emeritus.

Still fascinated by Russian politics, Spargo wrote several books, pamphlets and articles on Bolshevism, Karl Marx (his life and work), as well as the history of Vermont.

However, he never forgot his roots, and wrote a pamphlet on the Spargo name of Mabe, as well as an evocative poem (*below*) recalling his youth in his beloved Cornwall. John Spargo died in August 1966 and is interred in the Old Bennington Cemetery, Vermont.

A CORNISH LAD'S DAY

GORSE ABLOOM, A VAST GOLDEN SHEER;
A SKYLARK HIGH OUT OF SIGHT,
ITS JOYOUS SONG ECSTATIC, SWEET:
A DREAMING BOY TAKES HIS RIGHT!

A THROSTLE IN A MEDLAR TREE;
A PLOVER, IN FEAR-SPED FLIGHT;
WHITE DANCING CLOUDS, DARK RESTLESS SEA:
A VALIANT, TEN YEAR OLD KNIGHT!

WHITE FOAMING CRESTS ON BREAKERS TALL;
WILD SEA-MEWS THAT WHIRL AND SCREAM;
A CUCKOO'S FLUTE-TONED MATING CALL:
THE MAGIC OF A BOY'S DREAM!

FISH JUMPING IN THE WILLOWS' SHADE;
A MARLIN IN QUEST OF PREY;
A LAPWING'S NEST WITH CUNNING MADE:
A CORNISH LAD'S WELL-SPENT DAY!

Left to right: Bishop Reeves of Johannesburg, Dr J.B. Webb, G.K. Tucker Esq., Mrs W. Mountstephens and C.H. Leake Esq, JP, on the day the foundation stone was laid at St Stithians College Chapel.

Pritchard Street, Johannesburg, South Africa, 1931 (photo by Sir Bernard Stone).

ALBERT CHARLES COLLINS

Born at Menorlue into a devout Methodist family, Albert Charles Collins (*above*) attended Stithians School until leaving for employment with Mr Martin, carpenter and wheelwright at Hendra. He then moved to a Falmouth firm of builders incorporating an apprenticeship. Here he became a great friend with another apprentice, William Mountstephens, and the two young men made plans to emigrate to the United States. However, passengers leaving Plymouth for that part of the world were unfortunately delayed and they changed their plans and sailed, instead, on the *S.S. Teuton* to Capetown. From there they travelled to Kimberly, where, five years on, they were able to establish their own building business under the auspicious name of Mountstephens and Collins (Proprietary) Limited at Oriental Chambers, 36b Pritchard Street, Johannesburg. This was to become their permanent base. Albert Collins set up a company for his own personal interests and the two men prospered, providing financial aid for several enterprises in Pretoria and Johannesburg.

In the late 1920s the two friends provided the Falmouth and District Hospital in the (present) Trescobeas Road with the twelve-bed Mountstephens ward for males and the twelve-bed Collins ward for females as well as a children's ward of eight cots and an operating theatre, plus staff accommodation. Five years later the two men donated yet another sum. This resulted in the 'Freedom of the Borough' being conferred on them both, as well as the 'Freedom of the Borough' of Penryn. A freedom casket is on display in the Council Chambers.

President of the Stithians Agricultural Association in 1930, later in the 1930s, Albert Collins provided the money needed to allow the Stithians Parish Council to go ahead with plans to purchase three acres of glebe land, as well as the funds to provide all of the equipment for a playing field.

Albert Collins died in 1937 and was interred in the Braamfontein Cemetery, Johannesburg. After personal bequests, his will made provision for many beneficiaries, both in South Africa and in England, including Dr Barnardo's Homes, National Children's Homes, St Dunstans and the National Lifeboat Institution, as well as Falmouth and District Hospital and Truro Infirmary. While not forgetting the village of his birth, he made bequests to the Wesley Methodist Church and Sunday School at Hendra, the Playing Field and the Agricultural Association.

Some 16 kilometres north of Johannesburg, St Stithians College was built at a cost of £250 000. This was from the residue of Collins' and Mountstephens' combined estates – by now Mountstephens had died also – and building commenced in 1950 (see 'St Stithians College').

William Mountstephens

Jane Corey

Marathon Cycle Ride From John O'Groats to Lands End

Jane Corey, daughter of Mr and Mrs G.D. Corey of Carncrees Farm (where she was born), attended Stithians School and the Falmouth High School before going on to Reading University where she gained her BSc. in meteorology and physics. She was later employed in the Rainfall Department of South West Water Authority at Exeter. It was whilst she was there, in 1985, that she successfully completed a lone sponsored cycle ride for charity (with no back-up), from John O'Groats to Lands End, raising £1000 plus a further £200 for the Royal Devon and Exeter Kidney Unit Fund. She covered almost 1000 miles, staying overnight in youth hostels or campsites en-route, and meeting her own expenses along the the way.

Jane kept a daily journal in spite of adverse weather conditions which persisted for almost all of her journey. It makes very interesting reading, as, when she says, on Monday 29 July:

It was raining heavily when I left, but as I went on up towards the Cairngorms it became wetter and windier and colder. The road was busy, but there were frequent alternative parallel routes on the old road. In Aviemore it was raining steadily and I was given a donation when I stopped by the shops and also had a minor cycle repair done free of charge. Out in the country again a little boy next to his Dad's car held out 51p as I passed. Just outside Dalwhinnie, the highest village in Scotland, I stopped for a quick lunch and a cold, desolate place it was for a picnic. It stopped raining, but a cold, strong wind was blowing from behind and this practically lifted me over the Pass at the top of the hill. I admired the vast, dark, threatening hills covered with grey, scudding curtains and began the long descent to Blair Atholl where I camped free of charge.

Almost every day Jane spoke of getting a soaking in the rain, and the cold seems to have been ever present, even in August, as on the eighth day, Saturday 3 August, when she says: 'The morning was absolutely miserable with a strong, bitterly cold wind and frequent heavy showers.'

At the journey's end to meet Jane were her parents and relatives and friends from Stithians. Gifts included £50 from Trago Mills and Mr Jack Jeffrey, the then president of the Stithians Agricultural Association, presented her with a gift of £20 from the Association, as well as a personal donation.

Jane had met all of her own expenses and got rain soaked regularly on the journey. She had set out from John O'Groats in the rain and arrived at Lands End in the rain! She started out on Friday 26 July ending her journey on Thursday 8 August 1985.

A keen amateur photographer, Jane has had several beautiful photographs published in the Royal Meteorological Society's Calendar as well as in the *Western Morning News* newspaper. Her enthusiasm for meteorology was probably first engendered in headmaster Jack R. Williams' class at Stithians School when the pupils had to make their own rain gauges. Jane has never looked back and she was, for several years, the official weather person for the Stithians Agricultural Association, providing the Show's officials with accurate rainfall figures during the day should there have been a need to claim on insurance for loss of attendance owing to rain.

Top: *Jane, photographed in an Exeter street prior to setting out on her epic journey on Friday 21 June 1985 (© Express and Echo).*

Left: *Jane's certificate, proof that she completed the journey.*

Chapter 16: Groups and Organisations

WOMEN'S INSTITUTE

Stithians Women's Institute was established on 17 December 1936 and the first committee meeting took place in January 1937 when Mrs H.F. Gordon of Trevales House was elected President and Miss Janie Hellings was appointed Honorary Secretary. Membership rose from 36 to 48 in the first year. The late Mrs E.M. Phillips, a founder member and indefatigable community worker, penned a vibrant and fascinating tribute which appeared in the *Stithians Times* as the village WI's golden jubilee approached. This is an extract:

We belong to the largest Women's organisation in the country, with 350 000 members. The Movement started in Canada in 1897, and the first WI in the United Kingdom was formed in Wales in 1915. It is non party political and non sectarian, and the original aim was 'to improve the quality of rural life by means of the fuller education of the Countrywoman.' Every aspect of life interests us and we help numerous causes: we have a friendly, happy time at our Monthly Meetings, Group Meetings, County Meetings and National Events.

The formation of Stithians WI was due entirely to the efforts of Mrs Connie Gordon and her two sisters who had been Members of Sussex WI before coming to live at Trevales. At the beginning we were fortunate in having [their] experience, the use of their lovely garden and rooms... for many events, and the only women car drivers in the WI at that time.

Our yearly Programmes are interesting and varied, with a Speaker or a Demonstration of Art or Craft, one or two Competitions, a 'ROLL call' (from Cookery to anecdotes), Current events, vocal and dramatic items, and, of course, the inevitable cup of tea, with a rota of hostesses who supply 'lovely grub'. Our Speakers covered many subjects in early days: in wartime we had help with rations (anybody remember dried egg or coffee from parsnips?). Nowadays subjects are too numerous to be listed, and many, if given in early days, would have left eyebrows permanently raised, or caused an 'attack of the vapours'. Demonstrations, Arts, Crafts and many skills are most helpful, and we are always pleased to sample the results of the Cook's evening.

Where in early years a talk on 'London' or 'The Isle of Wight' was a highlight, now we have 'On a cruise ship to Russia' or 'My visit to Oberammergau'. We have an interest in the Social Services, Police work, Home Economics, First Aid, car maintenance, floral art, and many sporting themes, etc. etc. From our beginning we have entered competitions; locally, at County, and at National level. In 1938 several Members travelled to London (first time for some) to the National Handicraft Exhibition, at which we had an entry good enough to be accepted. We also have several Certificates for One Act Play competitions.

In six cases [our programmes] have been winners in the County Competition for the best series of programmes. We have had two firsts (County Cup), one second, one third, and two Certificates of Merit.

During the War Years we worked, and worked, and worked for all the War 'efforts'. 'Make do and Mend' was an eleventh commandment. We knitted for Victory on the idea of 'Lend to Defend'. AND WE MADE JAM. Oh, yes, we made jam. We picked hundreds of pounds of blackberries, and between 1941 and 1945 we made 5183 1bs of jam in Trevales kitchen. During these years, too, we dealt with all [600 of] the Evacuees who came to the village... plus many expectant Mothers.

More recently, Members have served on County Committees; attended a Royal Garden Party at Buckingham Palace (for the WI Golden Jubilee); in this Village Community we have had two Members elected to Stithians Parish Council, one rising to the office of Chairman. We visit places of interest... and at Community events we 'do the teas'.

As we approach our Golden Jubilee, we look back to our Founder Members. Ten of the 36 are still alive: Mrs A. Bassett (née Phillips), Mrs M. Bolitho, Mrs S. Green (née Porter), Mrs E. Hendy (née Jelbert), Mrs M. Ivey, Mrs J. Manhire, Mrs R. Martin, Mrs E.M. Phillips (née Henderson), Mrs K. Richards (née Holman) and Miss S.N. Richards. Some are not well enough to attend Meetings, others have left the district, one has been a Member since 1937.

I cannot end without a tribute to Miss Janie Hellings, who was our very efficient Secretary from our inauguration until her death in 1963, a total of 25 years. We shared her joy when she was awarded the BEM for her work with National Savings, but we sorrowed greatly at her passing. At our 21st Birthday Party in 1958, the incoming President described Miss Hellings as 'not only the backbone of Stithians WI but nearly all the other bones as well'. I salute Miss Hellings and... Mrs Connie Gordon and say to them, 'You built better than you knew'. We Members of Stithians W.I. consider ourselves to be the salt of the earth. We welcome new Members – perhaps to add spice to the salt – and we give you our motto for the next 50 years – 'Take your hats off to the past, take your coats off to the future.'

Top: *December 1957 and cause for celebration at the 21st anniversary held in the Village Hall. The beautiful cake, immaculate tables, flowers and atmosphere of the occasion defied the hall's austerity.*
Above: *In 1966/7 members gathered at one of the earliest meetings in their new venue at Stithians CP School.*

GROUPS AND ORGANISATIONS

Below: *In June 1987, in commemoration of the golden jubilee, Stithians WI presented a seat for the churchyard extension. Pictured here are the three husbands whose skills ensured the construction and installation of the gift. Left to right: Messrs David Burke, the late Brian Bury, Rex Pascoe.*

Above: *Spring 1997 and 60 years on for the WI in Stithians. Members move with the times and achieve their objective in the provision of a ramp to make access to the Village Hall simpler for pushchairs, wheelchairs and the disabled. Margaret Stephens (seated) is pictured cutting the ribbon to declare the ramp open and Noreen Williams unveiled the plaque on completion of the £1000 project. The sensitive and practical scheme is also celebrated by Peggy Pascoe and Elizabeth Downing.*

Above: *December, 1957. The President, Mrs Mary C. Williams, made a presentation to Miss Janie Hellings and expressed the thanks of members for her dedicated service as Honorary Secretary for 21 years. Mrs B.W. Knuckey also joined the happy occasion. Miss Hellings continued in her post for another six years until her death in 1963.*

Brownies

Left: *In the late 1960s there were no brownies in the village and girls over eight years of age had to join the Perran-ar-Worthal group. They had a wonderful time participating in a varied programme but inevitably the time came when Stithians needed its own pack. This photograph shows the 1st Perran-ar-Worthal Brownies: Crowning of the May Queen, 1966, in the beautiful gardens of Perran-ar-Worthal Vicarage by kind invitation of the vicar, the Revd J.R. Jose.*

The first brownie guide pack was founded in 1968 and was well supported by parents and a wonderful local association, the Friends of Guiding. Mrs Irene Broom, Guider of Perran-ar-Worthal, gave her time and advice which was invaluable to the leaders. Mrs Peggy Pascoe (Brown Owl) and Mrs Janet Ivey (Tawny Owl) were fortunate to have the enthusiasm and help of Miss Mary Jago, a young leader known affectionately as 'Pip'. This photograph is one of the earliest, taken in May 1968 in the grounds of Stithians CP School and records the Divisional Commissioner's visit.
Left to right, back: Mrs Cynthia Johnson (Divisional Commissioner), Mrs Peggy Pascoe (Brown Owl), Mrs Janet Ivey (Tawny Owl), Miss Mary Jago, 'Pip' (young leader);
4th row: Lesley Pascoe, Carole Symonds Lisbeth Crone, Felicity Prowse, Sarah Jackson, Hilary Martin, Janie Crone;
3rd row: Cheryl Taberer, Mandy Webber, Sandra Hooper, Lindsay Shingler, Karen Davie, Belinda Ivey, 2nd row: Marcia Trerise, Jackie Trerise, Eleanor Pascoe, Debbie Selby, Diane Richards, Helen Jackson; front: Helen Trerise, Brenda Tuffery, Wendy Carlyon, Joanna Biscoe, Susan Trerise.

Brownies, 1968

Left: *Summer Revels with a gypsy theme at Feock in July. Brown Owl demonstrates the art of making a besom. Left foreground, Lindsay Shingler; to the right, Eleanor Pascoe; centre, Belinda Ivey and Karen Davie; and in the background, Carole Symonds.*

Right: *In August the St Stythians Brownies made a trip to St Michael's Mount where, to their delight, they reaffirmed the Brownie Promise in the chapel, in the presence of Lord and Lady St Levan who made the visit so special. Roly, the King Charles spaniel, is the centre of attention in this photograph of Lady St Levan with the girls.*

Below: *The Brownies line up to show off their cheerful and imaginative creations at the District Revels in brilliant sunshine at Feock in July.*

Special Guide and Brownie Days

Left: *In 1970 the company joined 1200 guides in Truro Cathedral to give thanks on the 60th anniversary of the founding of the movement. Beginning with a welcome from the Bishop of Truro, the Rt Revd J.M. Key, the service was led by the young people. Members of the 1st St Stythians Company are pictured in the foreground as they enter Truro Cathedral's west door.*

At Christmas in 1968 every brownie took part in their first nativity play, later presented from the altar steps of St Stythians Church on the occasion of the St Feock District Carol Service. The brownies sent a donation to Mr Jack Williams, headteacher of Stithians CP School, towards the school's Annual Senior Citizens Party. The cast includes: the three shepherds: Mandy Webber, Brenda Tuffery and Lindsay Shingler; brownie singers: Marcia, Jackie and Helen Trerise, Carol Moyle, Debbie Selby, Sandra Hooper, Lisbeth Crone, Eleanor Pascoe, Julie Laffin, Cheryl Taberer, Carole Symonds and Wendy Carlyon; the star angel: Sarah Jackson; cherubs: Joanna Biscoe and Karen Davie; Mary: Belinda Ivey; Joseph: Lesley Pascoe; angels: Kim Roberts, Diane Richards and Jane Wood; three kings: Janie Crone, Felicity Prowse and Hilary Martin.

Guides and Brownies Out And About

Above: *In June 1970 brownies and guides dipped into their funds to travel to Penryn in the hope that they would catch a glimpse of HRH Prince Charles during his official visit to the town. He was welcomed by civic leaders and then walked over to talk informally to the various groups of young people who were both delighted and surprised. This charming photograph encapsulates the ripple of merriment caused by Prince Charles when he commented that he was aware that brownies sat under mushrooms! His Royal Highness was left in no doubt that St Stythians had a toadstool at the centre of their brownie ring!*

Below: *The brownies entered into the spirit of the Village Carnival as a 'Pack of Diamonds' in 1970, as their tribute to the 60th Anniversary of the Girl Guide Movement. Gerald and Phyllis Reed of Crellow Lane decorated the float with immense pleasure and excitement. The brownies even included their all-important toadstool and owl.*

Left: *From little acorns, oak trees grow. A pow-wow took place amongst the 22 brownies in 1970 when they wanted to mark both conservation year and the diamond jubilee of the movement. The idea of planting two trees appealed and permission was sought from the Playing Field Committee. The idea grew rapidly and a report in the* West Briton *declared 'Tree Planting Rush started by Brownies'. More than 60 Stithians people (aged 2-70) met at the Playing Field in the spring of 1971 to plant 27 trees. Most village organisations gave a tree and there were personal plantings for families and loved ones. The trees were planted on three sides of the field and seven-year-old Kim Harry planted the first of the brownies' trees followed by nine-year-old Kim Roberts – an honour the girls won from a lucky dip at 'pow-wow'.*

Guides

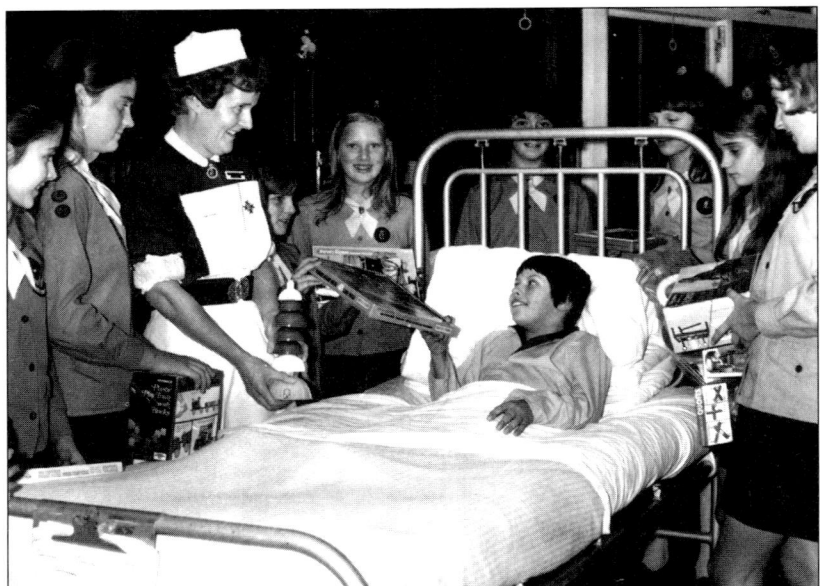

Left: *In November 1972 guides helped others less fortunate and they are seen presenting the results of their efforts to a young patient in the children's ward of the Royal Cornwall Hospital (City), Truro. The bright eyes and thoughtful expressions suggest that the challenge was worth while. Sister Ann Synge and her young patient accepted the gifts from Karen Davie, Caroline Morton, Lorna Smith, Julie Bennett, Jane Milan, Debbie Selby, Delia Morton and Belinda Ivey.*

The 1st St Stythians Guides on an outing in May 1973. Guides are responsible for organising their own programme of activities and a visit to the Air-Sea Rescue Service at the Royal Naval Air Station at Culdrose, Helston, was an exceptional learning experience during which 11-year-old Lorna Smith helped in a demonstration of the use of a life-jacket. The highlight of the tour was the inspection of the Whirlwind Search and Rescue Helicopter seen in this picture. Those present on the tarmac at Culdrose include: Guide Captain Janet Ivey, Julie Bennett, Delia Morton, Lorna Smith, Karen Davie, Deborah Smith, Linda Parkinson, Deborah Clegg, Jane Acton, Helen Trerise, Jane Milan, Caroline Morton, Belinda Ivey and Leading Airman Colin Simlett.

GROUPS AND ORGANISATIONS

In September 1985 the 1st St Stythians Guides completed a useful piece of community work in providing a tapped water supply to the churchyard extension. The guides rose to the challenge (set by their District Commissioner, Janet Ivey) of finding a project which would benefit the community whilst fulfilling the criteria for an application to the Royal Trusts Grant Scheme. Through their research they found that families, and especially elderly folk, had to carry water for the graves either from the old churchyard, negotiating a busy road, or bring water from home.

Organisations and parishioners were generous with support both practical and financial. The late Mr David Todd, retired South West Water Authority Manager, gave his help and advice which was invaluable. Mr Paul Gluyas of the Glebe Farm boosted hopes by suggesting that the supply could be taken from his water trough in the adjoining field thus avoiding the expense of breaking the road for a new supply pipe.

Mr Hugh Opie sent a mole plough to cut the 300-yard trench across the field to take the necessary piping and Mr H.L.C. Coode-Adams took on the difficult spade work beneath the hedges whilst Mr Clive Capp, the local plumber, worked on the connections.

The Royal Trusts donated £150 and the balance came from the Parish Council, Stithians Show, Penmennor Methodist Church, Marks and Spencer's Charity Fund, several business houses, individuals, the guides' own fund raising and interest whilst the money lay in the bank.

The guides presented their gifts with pride; they included the churchyard's new name plate in polished granite with gold lettering, together with a stone commemorating the project. The latter was given and prepared by Mr Rex Pascoe, whose wife, Peggy, was a long-serving guider in many senior capacities and who was the President of the splendid Local Association.

The guides planted two malus trees, one to mark the project and the other to celebrate the 75th year of guiding. They patiently planted spring bulbs in addition to saplings along the perimeter of the extension. In the photograph is the Revd (now Canon) Michael Warner who gave the company every encouragement and he is seen receiving the gifts together with a cheque towards the first year's water rate from Deborah Downing on behalf of the company!

Looking on are guiders Diane Richards and Teresa Pryor.

Guides

Left: *August 1973 saw the guides on board the* Scillonian *for a ten-day camp in the Isles of Scilly.*

Below: *Lorna Smith (back), Teresa Pryor and Deborah Smith enjoying their trip.*

Below left: *Deborah Smith and Caroline Morton.*

Right: *In December 1990 the company celebrated 21 years. A specially-made cake was cut by Mrs Peggy Pascoe and Mrs Joan Biscoe, founder guiders of the brownies and guides. Good works have continued down the years and in 1994, as their service to the community, the guides gave valuable help to the Village Hall by restoring the gardens. This involved sieving the earth, removing and carrying the stones (another good turn as this helped fill in some potholes elsewhere!) before digging in compost. In June 1994 the guides demonstrated their commitment by serving teas at the Village Hall to raise funds for shrubs. It is gratifying that a succession of dedicated guiders, friends of guiding, parents and supporters has ensured that both brownies and guides participate in this worthwhile organisation some 30 years on. Well done!*

GROUPS AND ORGANISATIONS

THE EVERGREENS

The members of this lively organisation for the over sixties have proved the aptness of the club's name. A varied programme includes excursions, guest speakers, outings, fund raising and entertainers which, combined with companionship and enthusiasm, demonstrate an outlook that is... ever green!

Left: *An important milestone – the Evergreens celebrate 21 years with a celebration lunch at the Royal Duchy Hotel, Falmouth.*

Above: *Another group at the same occasion.*

In the early 1970s the Evergreens pose for a photograph at their fête.

Top: *Stithians' St John Ambulance Division team with a shield which they won in London, 1946. Left to right, back: Serg. J. Hopper, R.L. Dunstan, R. Clifford, E.T. Tresidder; seated: Ambulance Officer O. Peters and Divisional Supt. R. Richards.*
Above: *Ladies Ambulance Committee fundraisers in the early 1940s. Left to right, standing: Miss L.J. Phillips, Mrs M. Spargo, Mrs Bache, Miss Janie Bowden, Mrs R. Martin, Mrs A. Moyle, Mrs E. Pascoe, Miss P. Phillips; seated: Miss Norah Way, district nurse, Mrs L. Mitchell, Mrs E.M. Phillips, Mrs J. Bowden, Mrs Harvey, Miss B. Knuckey.*
Above right: *the Brigade's fund-raising victory calendar of 1944.*

St John Ambulance Brigade

Residents of Stithians have had a long association with the St John Ambulance but it has never been recorded. The minutes of the first meeting were recorded on 22 October 1930 when the Carnmenellis Division was formed and they met in the canteen of the Polhigey Mine which had recently been re-opened. Commissioner Edgar Trounson attended and explained the objects and aims of the organisation, the Div. Surgeon was to be Dr G. Robinson and the Supt. Mr R.J. Willoughby (the mine captain). Ambulance Officer was W.J. Phillips and F. Negus was Sergeant.

By October 1932, when their annual report and appeal letter was sent out, they stated that they had conveyed 27 patients to and from hospital, and that they had treated 81 cases requiring first aid. The section had been enlarged with qualified personnel from Stithians (men and women), as well as cadets from Carnmenellis. The report was signed by William J. Phillips, Supt. S.T. Bowden and Ambulance Officer J. Murton (Secretary) and W. Mills (Treasurer). President was J.S. Richards of Auburn House, Stithians, Vice Presidents were E. Tresidder of Hill Crescent, Carnmenellis, and W.J. Andrew of Crellow, Stithians. This is when the brigade became the Carnmenellis and Stithians Division.

In 1939 the order bought the small chapel at Foundry, Stithians, from W.J.T. Peters, a builder who had used it as a workshop. This then became the headquarters.

Top: *Polhigey mine, Carnmenellis, which re-opened in 1930. The Brigade was needed in case of any accidents at the mine (Cornish Studies Library, Redruth).*

Above: *The Prince of Wales when he visited the mine in 1930. Polhigey was the first place in the district to be connected with electricity.*

Right: *Dedication of a converted ambulance for the Carnmenellis and Stithians Division in 1940. It was a maroon Daimler automatic and had been owned by a doctor in Penzance. Supt. S.T. Bowden and Ambulance Officer Oscar Peters were in charge and it was used in the area for many years.*

Top: *The Nursing Division of the St John Ambulance Brigade in Stithians in 1940. Left to right, standing: Doris Downing, Bessie Bath, June Gardner, Marjory Richards, Laura Richards, Doreen Toy; front: Annie Moyle, Janie Hellings, Supt. Florence Wills, Sadie Porter, Joyce Andrew, Gwen Spargo.*
Above: *In 1980 there were 55 members of the local St John Ambulance cadet division. Here five of the cadets are receiving awards. Left to right: Christopher Hooper, Shaun Charles, Duane Bullocke, Helen Bowden and Jacqui Keep.*

Chapter 17: Sport and Entertainment

Shop Pool Carnival was a highlight of the leisure activities in Stithians in times past. The following report of the 1934 carnival appeared in the *Penryn Advertiser* of 17 August 1934:

CARNIVAL KING?

There were 17 candidates for the title of Carnival Queen of Shop Pool, Stithians, and the judges, Capt. and Mrs J.C. Annear, Penryn, selected Miss Joyce Dunstan as the 'Queen', and the Misses Marjorie Bath, Gladys Lewis, Doreen Spargo and Nancy Martin as her attendants. They were all typically English country girls, and they (the judges) gave their decision entirely on those lines. Capt. Annear suggested the committee should select a 'Carnival King', as this is seldom, if ever, done in Carnivals.

Above: *Shop Pool/Goonlaze Carnival, c.1938. Left to right: Roy Trerise, Betty Julian, Enid Prowse, Gordon Hall, Pearl Drew, Peter Phillips.*

Shop Pool/Goonlaze Carnival, c.1932. This event was usually held during Feast Week and started at Goonlaze with a band parading through the village and back again for the prize-giving.
Left to right, standing: E.M. Henderson, L. Pascoe, H. Manhire, C. Martin, A. Dunstan, S. Bowden; seated: F. Gluyas, R. Martin, A. Pascoe, J. Gluyas, V. Bowden. This float depicts a school scene.

Stithians Rugby Club, 1938/9.
Left to right, back: Jack Simmons, Raymond Gluyas, Leonard Knuckey, Eddie Brown, Morley Trerise, Fred Dunstan, Glenwood Odgers, Jack Knuckey, Arnold Pascoe;
centre: Tom Penaluna, Jack Eddy, Godfrey Spargo, Ivor Andrew, Bobby Trerise, Arnold Burley, Reg Dunstan;
front: Claude Knuckey, Willie Clark.

Stithians Rugby Club, 1946/47.
Left to right, back: Telfer Pascoe (committee member), Vivian Downing, Glenwood Odgers, Joe Andrew, William Britton (committee member), Ivor Andrew, Wilfred Prowse (committee member), Vivian Cleave, Jack Odgers, Desmond Burley, Frank Trerise (committee member);
centre: John Knuckey, Nicholas Pascoe (committee member), Arnold Burley, Godfrey Spargo, Roy Sweet;
front: Dennis Cossentine, Roy Trerise, Fred Dunstan, Jack Floyd, Tom Penaluna, Roy Pascoe.

SPORT AND ENTERTAINMENT

Boy's Football Team c. 1930.
Left to right, back: Bob Wills (coach), John Noye, Andrew Stumbles, Willie Clark, Vivian Downing, Edgar Treloar, Sam Annear (coach);
front: Bobbie Trerise, Glenwood Odgers, Norman Williams, Kenneth Mead, Fred Dunstan.

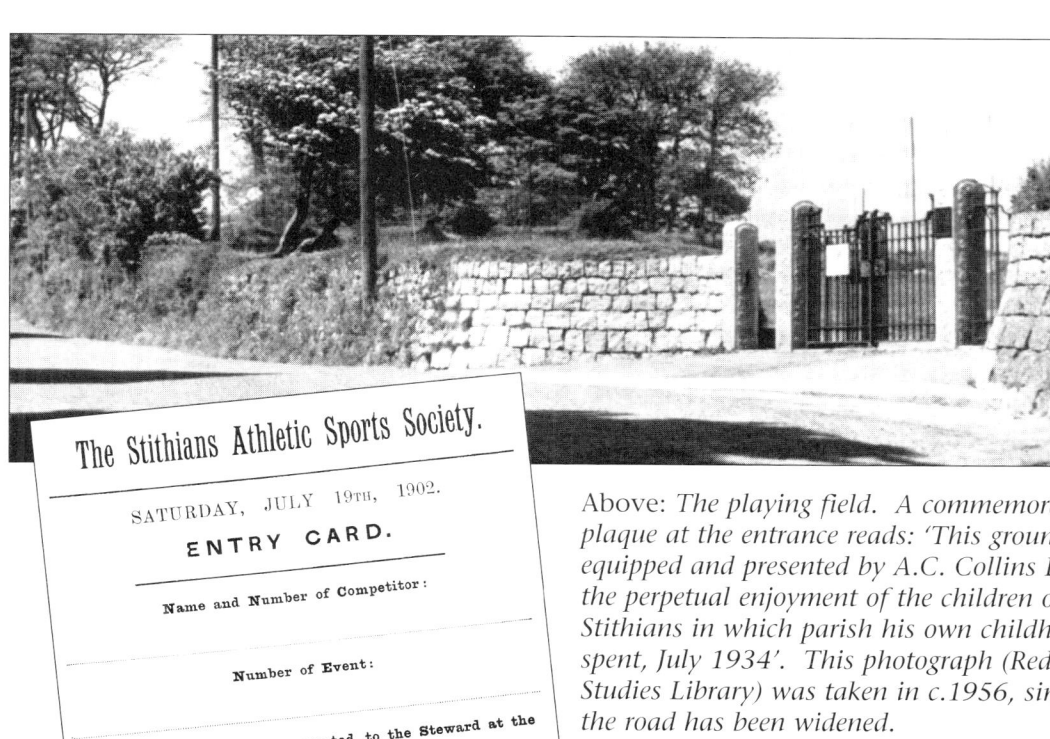

Above: *The playing field. A commemorative plaque at the entrance reads: 'This ground was equipped and presented by A.C. Collins Esq., for the perpetual enjoyment of the children of Stithians in which parish his own childhood was spent, July 1934'. This photograph (Redruth Local Studies Library) was taken in c.1956, since when the road has been widened.*

Left: *A printed entry card for the Stithians Athletic Sports Society. Athletic sports were held for many years in the show field on Feast Saturday.*

A scene from the production of The Holly and The Ivy, *1952.
This was perhaps the most popular play in Stithians.*

The cast takes a bow at the end of And This Was Odd *against a festive backdrop, November 1953.
Left to right: Gerard Kelly, Janet Reed, Will Pascoe, Margaret Kneebone, Peggy Pascoe, Christine Andrew,
Bettie Phillips, Margery Pascoe, Allan Smith.
Inset: A scene from the play with (left to right): Will Pascoe, Gerard Kelly,
Janet Reed and Margaret Kneebone.*

Stithians Amateur Dramatic Society

Amateur dramatic societies flourished in the early 1950s and Stithians was no exception! Stithians' society had begun in 1952 with the following officers: Chairman and Producer, Jack R Williams; Hon. Secretary, Rex Pascoe; Hon. Treasurer, John C. Harris; Stage Managers, Ivor Andrew and Bernard Martin; Property Mistresses, Margery Pascoe and Margaret Phillips; Wardrobe Mistress, Bettie Phillips; Prompter, Dorothy Briddon.

They met at the former Unionist Hall in New Road using a lower room. The cramped space did not put a stop to rehearsals and the fact that premises were in a decrepit state shows that members were certainly determined to achieve their aim. Many splendid productions were staged in the Church Hall under the energetic and talented direction of Jack Williams, whose vision enabled the society to feature well-written and worthwhile plays. The society was received enthusiastically by the village and there were excellent attendances on the presentation of the first production, *No Medals*, a three-part comedy by Esther McCracken, with a cast of 11. The drama, *The Holly and The Ivy* by Wynard Browne, was another successful venture, playing in December 1952 to full houses.

Above: *A scene from* The Holly and the Ivy. *Left to right: Michael Andrew (Nick Gregory), Betty Pearce (Margaret Gregory), Will Pascoe (Richard Wyndham), Peggy Pascoe (Jenny Gregory), Bettie Phillips (Aunt Bridget), Jack Williams (Revd Martin Gregory) and Joan Noyes (Aunt Lydia). Ken Andrew (playing David Paterson) was off stage.*

Below: *The dress rehearsal of* No Medals *in May 1952. Left to right, back: Allan Smith, Eleanor Martin, Jack Williams, Janet Reed, Bettie Phillips, Michael Andrew, Will Pascoe; front: Peggy Pascoe, Christine Andrew, Mary Williams, Barbara Smith.*

St Stythians Male Voice Choir, 1951.
Left to right, back: Fred Dunstan, Tom Penaluna, Leonard Evans, Roy Pascoe, Harry Dunstan, Tom Penaluna senr;
5th row: Roy Mitchell, Jack Pascoe, Percy Duff, Will Bowden, Arnold Burley;
4th row: Redvers Pellow, Clifford Dunstan, Will Odgers, Jack Simmons, Godfrey Spargo;
3rd row: Dennis Pearce, Ken Pooley, Cresswell Spargo, Kenneth Mead, Garfield Eddy, Freddy Duff;
2nd row: Percy Moyle, Victor Pascoe, Jack Pearce, Will Pascoe, Willie Bache, Horace Dunstan;
front: Charlie Nicholls, Wilfred Prowse, Betty Gluyas (pianist), Sydney Bowden (conductor), Tom Prowse, Thomas James Andrew, Cecil Mead.

St Stythians Silver Band outside the garage at the rear of Pencrellow, New Road – then the home of Frank and Janie Gluyas, c.1945.
Left to right, back: Denman Dunstan, Raymond Gluyas, Alfie Opie, George Robinson, Eddie Brown, Norman Tregenza, Lloyd Sarah, Harry Lockwood;
centre: Frank Knuckey, Jack Pascoe, Eddie Sanders, Jack Burleigh, Vivian Downing, Bernard Martin, Will Bowden, Gus Davey, Rex Manhire, Kitchener Dunstan, Claude Knuckey (drum);
front: Gordon Jenkin, Jim Eustace, Jack Knuckey, Edgar Floyd (conductor), Frank Gluyas, Wilfred Prowse, Leonard Rosevear, Charlie Eustace, Eric Trerise, Reggie Dunstan.

MUSIC

Music has long played a major role in the social life of Stithians. In the late 1800s there were choirs at St Stythians Parish Church, Hendra Methodist Chapel and Penmennor Methodist Chapel. There was also a Fife and Drum Band though little is known of its formation. It was certainly in existence in 1885 for it is recorded in the minutes of Penmennor Sunday School for July of that year: '... that we have two bands on Feast Tuesday: Dunstan's Fife and Drum Band and a cheap brass band'. Penmennor Sunday School also invited the band to play at its tea treat in 1902, though on this occasion it was referred to as Stithians Fife and Drum Band.

Conductor of the Fife and Drum Band was William Henry Dunstan, a stonemason. The late Sydney Bowden penned a description of Mr Dunstan's method of conducting:

He would stand in the middle of his 15 or so musicians playing his own fife and nodding his head to keep the other flautists and the drummers in time.

The Fife and Drum Band was in great demand during the First World War when its repertoire included folk songs, patriotic songs (such as 'Keep the Home Fires Burning' and 'Tipperary'), and a few Sankey hymns.

St Stythians Silver Band was formed at a meeting in the Parish Institute in 1928. Mr Tom Penaluna, who had been a playing member of Rame Cross Band, was appointed the first conductor. It is interesting to note that of the 29 men who joined the band, only one, Mr W.J. Treloar, had played an instrument before. A deputation to the Bugle Band Contest resulted in the purchase of a set of 29 instruments from Bessons & Co., on which a Welsh band had defaulted.

Stithians Hendra Methodist Chapel granted permission for the band to practice in its little meeting house in East Road. This was to be the practice room for 40 years and the band purchased the property in 1930 for £60. In 1965 the band started actively looking for a site for a new band room. A site about 60 yards from the old one was acquired and the building firm of W. Prowse & Son was engaged to erect the building. The new room (still in use) was officially opened on 20 April 1968 by Alderman K.G. Foster, CBE, JP, Chairman of Cornwall County Council.

Gribbes Chapel after it had been closed and bought by St Stythians Silver Band. They are seen here marching out after the redecoration of the building.

The first known minute book for St Stythians Male Voice Choir dates from 7 May 1919. It was the tradition for men from the village to gather and go around the houses singing carols at Christmas time and it was these men who formed the nucleus of the choir. At first the choir walked to neighbouring towns and villages to give their concerts but at a meeting on 6 October 1919 'It was decided that we accept no invitation over a radius of three miles to walk: over that distance, we ride'.

The year 1920 saw the choir giving 35 concerts and raising over £350 for charity. However, there was a decrease in attendance at the practices in 1921 and in 1925 practices were stopped for 12 months. When the choir was called together again in October of 1926, only five people turned up and a decision was taken to 'close down indefinitely'.

There was a resurgence of interest after the Second World War and at a meeting in the Unionist Hall on 23 January 1947, St Stythians Male Voice Choir was re-formed. It soon began competing in music festivals, something that was to be a major activity for the choir for the next 20 years. During that period the choir sang in 35 festivals, winning 15 first, 10 second and 5 third prizes. From 1967 the choir did less festival work, concentrating instead on concerts. St Stythians Male Voice Choir continues to thrive.

Also thriving is Stithians Ladies Choir which was formed in 1966. Its origins are interesting. The choir at Penmennor Methodist Chapel (now Stithians Methodist Church) was struggling in 1966 due to a shortage of male singers. Faced with this problem, the then organist and choirmaster,

Drayton Ladies Choir (photo by T.P. Roskrow, Truro).
Left to right, back: Jane Davey (pianist), Margaret Bowden, Valerie Collins, Jean Bowden, Ann Andrew, Peggy Phillips, Betty Gilkes, Netta Andrew, Kathleen Clemens;
3rd row: Lee Prowse, Margaret Waters, Pam Thomas, Margaret Reed, Mary Clemens, Margaret Phillips, Mary Williams, Phyllis Gluyas;
2nd row: Daiseen Marshall, Lucille Combellack, Enid Waters, Christine Andrew, Mavis Pascoe, Rosemary Downing, Bernice Nicholls;
front: Betty Pearce, Marjorie Pascoe, Marlene Eddy, Ken Drayton (conductor), Shirley Thomas, Rosemary Smith, Gloria Stapelton.

Stithians Ladies Choir, 1968 (photo Robert Roskrow, Truro).
Left to right, back: Valerie Tresidder, Mamie Rowe, Winnie Trevena, Betty Paget, Ivy Eddy, Janet Gluyas, Mavis Collins, Jean Gluyas, Marlene Eddy, Christine Poad, Heather Berryman, Rosemary Evans, Pat Rowe, Olive Webber;
3rd row: Marlene Barlow, Heather Dunstan, Lorna Opie, Gwennie Spargo, Lee Bowden, Margaret Stephens, Jean Pope, Lorna Pascoe, Angeline Pascoe, Marlene Pascoe, Thelma Trerise, Edna Olds;
2nd row: Yvonne Peters, Peggy Pascoe, Betty Burleigh, Pam Bearham, Olive Pooley, Phyllis Gluyas, Bernice Bearham, Mildred Andrew, Gwennie Nicholls, June Bache, Jean Andrew, Ann Trerise, Barbara Mead, Mary Jeffery, Diane Pascoe;
front: Aileen Webb, Caroline Opie, Kathryn Mead, Margaret Bolitho, Betty Gluyas (accompanist), Sydney Bowden (conductor), Joan Biscoe, Margery Pascoe, Marjorie (Bath) Pascoe, Violet Bowden, Sally Roberts.

Mr Sydney Bowden, arranged a programme with ladies' voices for the annual Harvest Festival concert. The event was such a success that a fortnight later a special meeting was called and Stithians Ladies Choir was created.

It quickly established a high reputation for itself and has had considerable success both with festival work and with its concert programme. It has made a number of recordings, including a highly popular series of albums featuring Sankey hymns made jointly with St Stythians Male Voice Choir.

Over the years Stithians has produced other choirs. In the 1920s Mr John Gluyas, caretaker of Penmennor Methodist Chapel, formed a Band of Hope male choir. This was based at the chapel and was in popular demand. When this group ceased in 1930, a number of its members formed the Penmennor Glee Singers. They were: Sydney Bowden, Ken Mead, Will Odgers, Will and Victor Pascoe, Cresswell Spargo, Norman Tregenza, and Bobbie and Morley Trerise. They engaged Mr H. Dennis, the organist at Redruth Wesley Chapel (now Redruth Methodist Church), as their trainer and gave countless concerts throughout Cornwall until the war forced them to disband in 1941. They were assisted at most engagements by soloist Eileen Kemp and elocutionist Pat Mitchell.

During his short stay in Stithians Mr Ken Drayton made a considerable impact on the musical life of the parish. A talented musician, he joined the teaching staff of Stithians School in 1948. He formed a school choir which gave concerts in Stithians and neighbouring villages, and in c.1950 broadcast on national radio on the BBC 'Children's Hour' programme.

In May 1950 Mr Drayton formed the Drayton Ladies Choir which undertook both concert and festival work. In its first year it won 5th place at the Camborne Music Festival. When Mr Drayton left Stithians in 1952 to take up an appointment as headmaster of a school in Dorset, he was succeeded as conductor by Mrs M. Evans of Camborne. Under her baton, the choir, in the words of the late Mr Sydney Bowden, 'attained a very high standard indeed'. However, Mrs Evans was only with the choir for a short time as she left to join her husband overseas. Shortly afterwards the Drayton Ladies Choir disbanded.

The Penmennor Glee Singers, c.1930.
Left to right, standing: Will Pascoe, Kenneth Mead, Eileen Kemp, Creswell Spargo,
Kenneth Bowden, Bobbie Trerise, Morley Trerise;
kneeling: Sidney Bowden, Will Odgers.

St Stythians Silver Band, c.1930, photographed at Shop Pool (Goonlaze) before the band had uniforms.
Left to right, back: Claude Knuckey, Leonard Williams, Roy Sarah, Billy Treloar, Sam Annear, Redvers Phillips, Stuart Andrew, Reggie Dunstan, Casper Andrew, Clifford Dunstan, Cecil Mead;
centre: Wilfred Prowse, Lloyd Sarah, Garfield Knuckey, Harry Andrew, Arnold Knuckey, Howard Phillips, ?, John Charles Williams, Garfield Collins, Raymond Bath, Kitchener Dunstan, Percy Spargo;
front: Joe Williams, Norman Tregenza, Bob Tresidder, Eddie Brown, Tom Penaluna (conductor), Lewis Trerise, Charlie Andrew, Will Bowden.

Chapter 18: Views of Stithians Old and New

If you take in the panoramic view of Stithians from the top of Goonorman hill (540ft) and look north west, with Carnmenellis on your left and Carnmarth on your right, the village of Stithians is in the foreground. The individual hills are separated by relatively broad valleys – a view which is representative of the whole region. To some extent the obtruding spurs restrict views up and down the valleys, resulting in the isolation of villages from one and another. In the early days this characteristic of the landscape tended to foster a strong village and parish individuality akin to clannishness. Before the improvement of transport, the economic and cultural life, as well as the physical view of the inhabitants, was confined to a small area by the nature of these enclosing hills and ridges. Villages like Stithians, Mabe, Lanner and Wendron were equally separate and individual in their cultural life. The village of Crellow, as it was called in the old days, consisted of New Road, Crellow Lane, Crellow Fields, South Road, Tregonning Road (leading to Trevales) and East Road leading down to Foundry.

If you go up to the church, one road leads to Sewrah Mill and Trembroath, and the other leads to Hendra Close, Hendra Terrace, Hendra Farm and on past the two chapels to the little hamlet of Goonlaze. Still continuing on the road to Redruth, you come to another part of the village, Penhalvean. The road to the reservoir is here and that leads to Penmarth and Carnmenellis. Taking the south road in the village, you pass Tretheague, Trewince, Menerdue, Rosemanowes and join the Helston-Falmouth road to pass through Longdowns which is found at the end of the parish.

An aerial view of the village taken in the late 1960s showing the new council houses in Collins Park and the road leading down to Foundry, with Kennall Vale in the distance.
(Photo by permission of the Commanding Officer, RNAS Culdrose.).

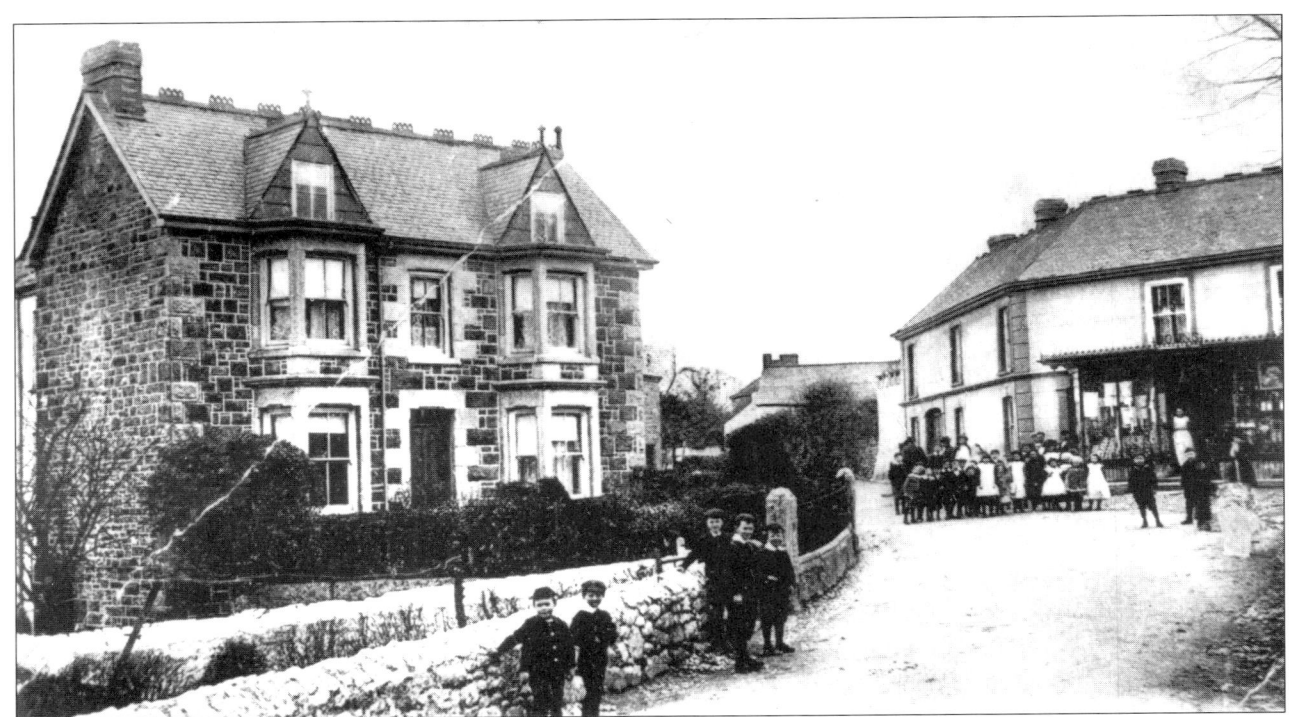

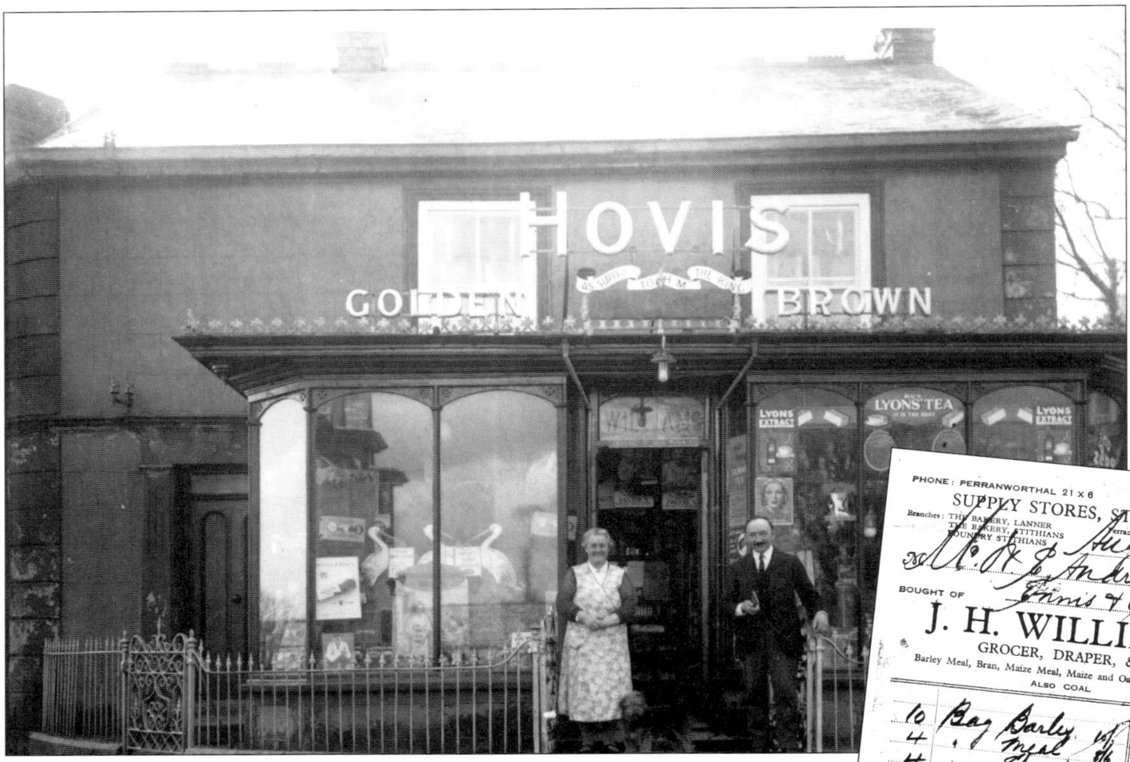

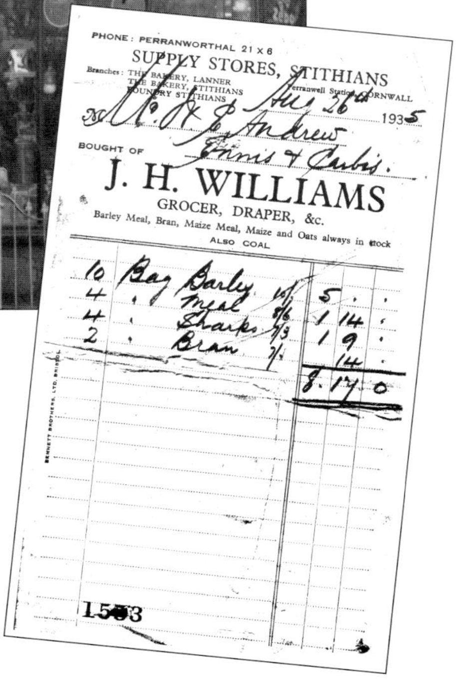

PHONE: PERRANWORTHAL 21 X 6
SUPPLY STORES, STITHIANS
Branches: THE BAKERY, LANNER; THE BAKERY, STITHIANS; FOUNDRY STITHIANS — Perranwell Station, CORNWALL
Mr R. J. Andrew — Aug 26th 1935
BOUGHT OF
J. H. WILLIAMS
GROCER, DRAPER, &c.
Barley Meal, Bran, Maize Meal, Maize and Oats always in stock
ALSO COAL

10	Bag Barley	10/	5	.
4	" Meal	8/6	1 14	.
4	" Sharps	9/3	1 9	.
2	" Bran	7/	14	
			8 17 0	

1503

Top: *The centre of the village, often referred to as Trefalgar Square.*

Above: *Mr and Mrs Joe Williams outside their Supply Stores in the early 1930s. In those days there were five shops in the village, supplying groceries and bread. Today this is the only one left and is run by Londis.*

Right: *A bill showing that they also sold coal and feed stuffs to the local farmers.*

VIEWS OF STITHIANS OLD AND NEW

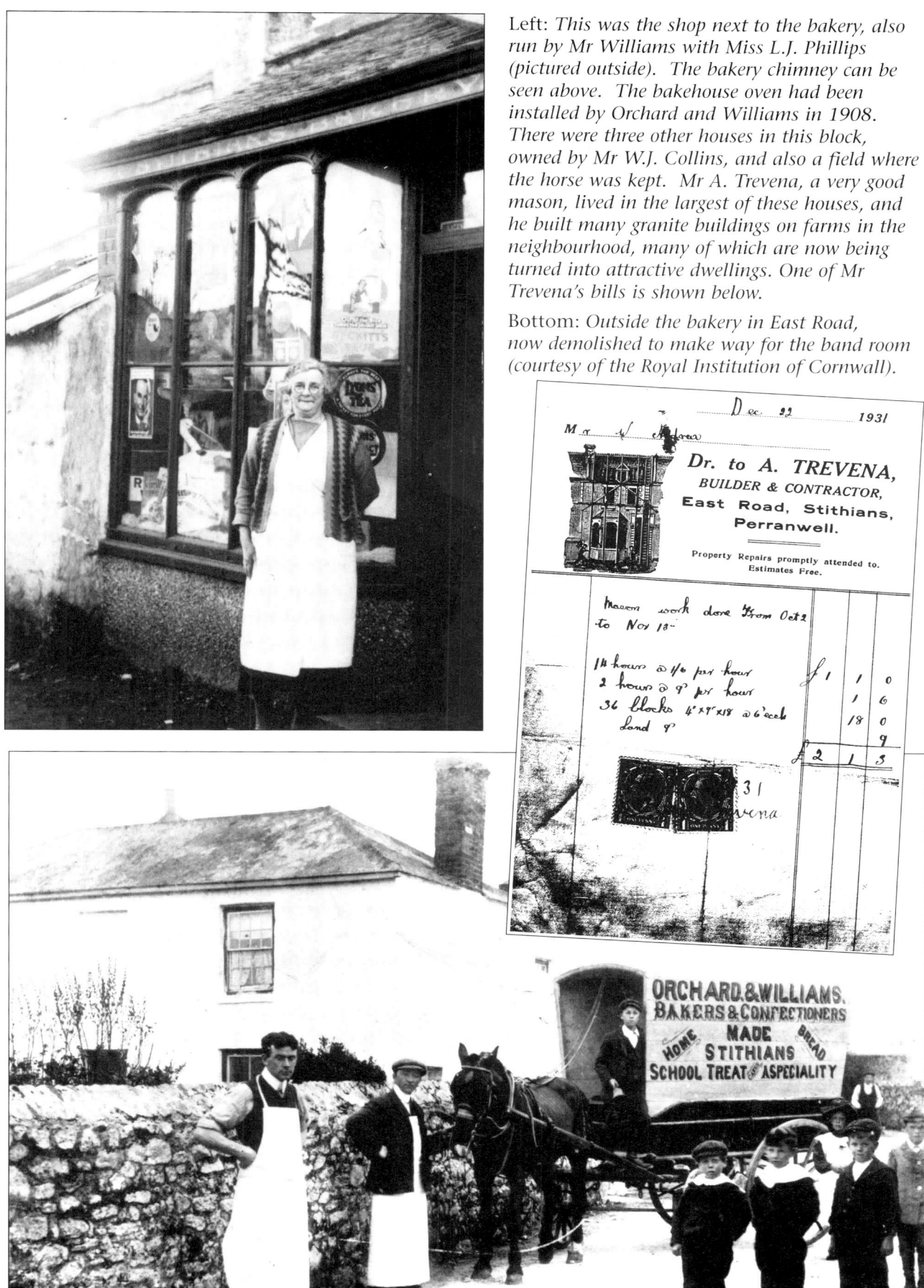

Left: *This was the shop next to the bakery, also run by Mr Williams with Miss L.J. Phillips (pictured outside). The bakery chimney can be seen above. The bakehouse oven had been installed by Orchard and Williams in 1908. There were three other houses in this block, owned by Mr W.J. Collins, and also a field where the horse was kept. Mr A. Trevena, a very good mason, lived in the largest of these houses, and he built many granite buildings on farms in the neighbourhood, many of which are now being turned into attractive dwellings. One of Mr Trevena's bills is shown below.*

Bottom: *Outside the bakery in East Road, now demolished to make way for the band room (courtesy of the Royal Institution of Cornwall).*

An early view of New Road, c.1900, before Mr Gluyas' shop was built.

Above: *Mr Frank Gluyas' shop in New Road where he sold sweets, hardware, petrol (the old pump is on the left of the photograph), and new bicycles – he repaired them too. The trophies in the window had been won by the St Stythians Silver Band. Mr Gluyas also ran a taxi service.*

Left: *Bill from Frank Gluyas for a new burner for a primus, which many people used before they had electricity.*

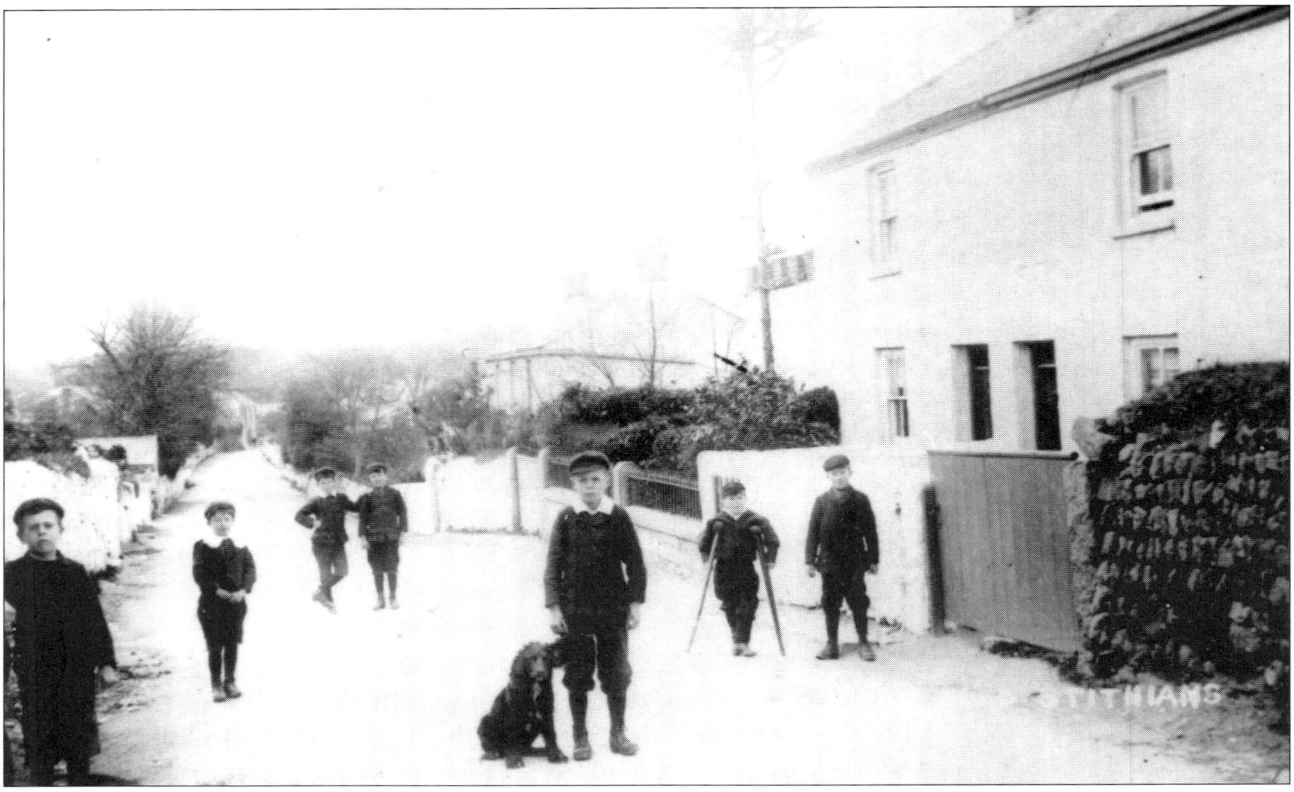

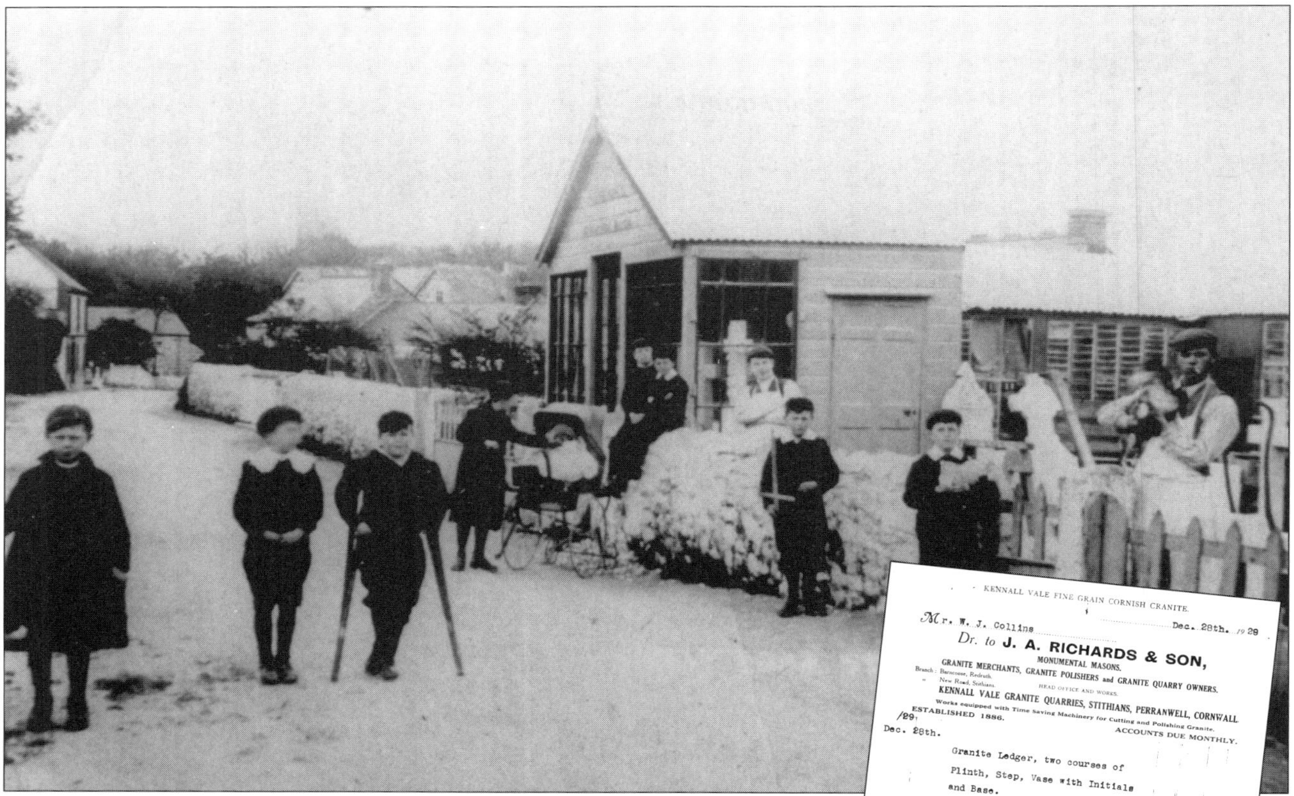

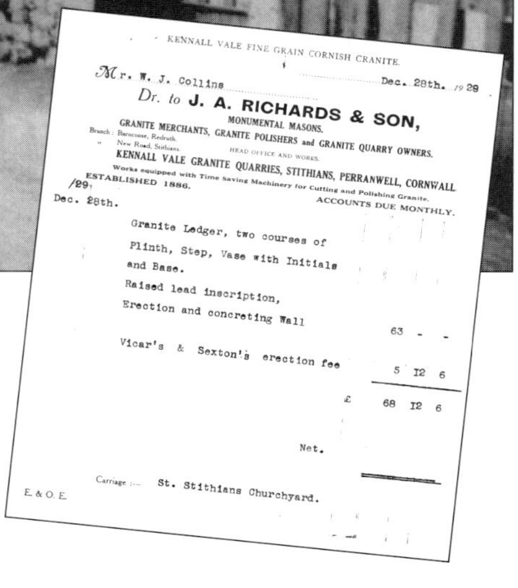

KENNALL VALE FINE GRAIN CORNISH CRANITE.

Mr. W. J. Collins .... Dec. 28th. 1929

Dr. to **J. A. RICHARDS & SON,**

MONUMENTAL MASONS.

GRANITE MERCHANTS, GRANITE POLISHERS and GRANITE QUARRY OWNERS.

Branch: Barncoose, Redruth.
" New Road, Stithians.

HEAD OFFICE AND WORKS.

KENNALL VALE GRANITE QUARRIES, STITHIANS, PERRANWELL, CORNWALL.

Works equipped with Time Saving Machinery for Cutting and Polishing Granite.

ESTABLISHED 1886.

ACCOUNTS DUE MONTHLY.

/29
Dec. 28th.

Granite Ledger, two courses of Plinth, Step, Vase with Initials and Base. Raised lead inscription, Erection and concreting Wall	63	-	-
Vicar's & Sexton's erection fee	5	I2	6
£	68	I2	6
Net.			

Carriage :— St. Stithians Churchyard.

E. & O. E.

Top: *Another view of New Road, looking in the same direction as the picture on page 140, but nearer Gribbes Corner.*

Above: *These were the cutting sheds and showroom of J.A. Richards' granite works before they were removed to Kennall Vale.*

Right: *A bill from J.A.Richards & Son showing offices at New Road, as above, and Barncoose, Redruth.*

VIEWS OF STITHIANS OLD AND NEW

Left: *Stithians Unionist Club in New Road, built in 1913, and opened by Mrs J.C. Williams, wife of the local Member of Parliament at that time. The opening ceremony was followed by tea and a concert and Mr E.J. Rodda was Chairman. Thanks were recorded to those who assisted in the erection of the building by Mr J.T. Peters and seconded by Mr J.A. Richards. They had received help from many directions and Sir Edwin and Lady Durning-Lawrance and Mr Opie (who had sent a subscription from New Zealand) were mentioned. The foundation stones had been laid by Charles Williams, Sir E. Durning-Lawrance, Lady Durning-Lawrance, Capt W.F. Tremayne, J.T. Peters and J.T. Collins (secretaries), J. Davies-Gilbert, G.T. Thomas-Peter, J.C. Williams, and also the Stithians Ladies' Unionist Association and the Stithians Men's Unionist Association. This was reported in the Penryn Advertiser on 12 December 1913. The building was used for many years for concerts, whist drives and horticultural shows, and in the basement there was a billiard table. Mr Harold Phillips was the last treasurer. It is now a private house.*

Above: *This was the home of a very talented man, Mr John T. Collins, a mason by trade who was Secretary of the Unionist Association and gave 'magic lantern' shows in the house and wrote poetry. At one stage this was three houses but is now one and is owned by Mrs Dorothy Parsons. It has always been called Ivydene and is in New Road.*

Truro-Helston Division Unionist Song.

Tune—"Trelawny."

"UP CHARLIE!"

Electors all, when comes the call
  To fight in "Union's Cause,"
The "Cause" of true prosperity,
  Of just and equal laws;
The "Cause" that says "Tis England first."
  "Britain SHALL rule the sea;"
"Let British men do England's work,
  Helped by each Colony."

CHORUS.

Then "One and All" for "Williams" Vote,
  And let opponents see,
For Unions Cause and righteous laws,
  Our Member he shall be.

The Rads have tried with Chinese Slaves,
  And German Bread so black,
Big Loaves, and Old Age Pension lies,
  To keep our prestige back;
They say, "You've Labour Bureaus now,
  No longer need you shirk—"
ONE THOUSAND CLERKS ARE THERE MAINTAINED,
  But alas!—there is no work.

CHORUS.

The Irish clamour for Home Rule,
  While Asquith tears his hair,
And Lloyd George still of "hen roosts" dreams,
  And Churchill says, "O dear."
I fear our prestige is all gone,
  But list to what we teach—
If people hiss our politics,
  Why go around and preach?

CHORUS.

Then up, ye bands of Unionists,
  Fight on, with heart and hand,
With truth to guide us in the fray,
  Let's altogether stand
Shoulder to shoulder every man,
  "Tariff Reform" our cry,
And Cornwall's Charlie we'll return,
  Or know the reason why.

CHORUS.

J. T. COLLINS,
Hon. Secretary, Stithians Unionist Association.

Printed and Published by Netherton & Worth, Lemon Street, Truro.

Song by Mr John T. Collins on a political theme.

Top: *Tozer's shop (listed in* Kelly's Directory, *1902). John Tozer was a shop-keeper and James and John Tozer were bootmakers. Later Mrs Hall ran the shop and her brother also helped. For several years it has been a fish and chip shop. Note the earthenware water pitchers in the road.*

Above: *This is Gribbes Corner, c.1900, with the pump, which is where Mr W.J. Opie used to come on a weekly basis for two earthenware pitchers of water, all the way from Redruth. He was not the only one who thought that the spring water was better than any from a town reservoir. (sketch by Ruth Berriman)*

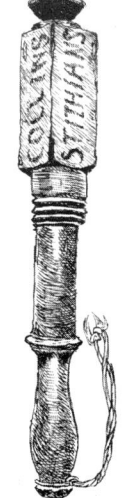

Above: *Another view of Gribbes Corner, early 1900s, with Mrs Eva's shop on the left and beyond that Billy Connibeare's house, which was later demolished. Billy was quite a character in the village, as he was so small. Mr and Mrs W.J.T. Peters ran the shop for many years, followed by others, but now the building has been converted into two flats and a hairdressing salon. Mrs L. Ford, now aged 103 years, with the basket on the left of the picture, is with her late sister Charlotte.*

Left: *A typical granite cottage of the Victorian era. This one shows Mr Edwin Trerise's mother and grandmother outside their home, which was later joined with two others to become the Police House in South Road. There was a resident policeman in Stithians for many years.*

Right: *The constables' staff was used in c.1850 by Peter Collins (whose name it bore). He was born at Goonvean and had a shop in Stithians before moving to Devon.*

VIEWS OF STITHIANS OLD AND NEW

Left: *The old cottages in East Road where members of the Burley and Bennetts families lived. The buildings were demolished in the 1970s and the long gardens in the front shortened to allow for the widening of the road.*

Right: *Rose Cottages, as they are called today, are a very pleasant feature in the village.*

Left: *Alma Terrace was sold by J.C. Williams in 1905 to William Eva at the shop. When he died in 1916, he left the property to his daughter, Mary Ann, who married William Francis Eslick and went to live in Butte, Montana, USA. In 1918 Nicholas Pascoe of Vellandrucia bought the four cottages from her (and the large gardens at the back) for £212. In more recent years, another cottage has been built on the end and houses have been built on the gardens.*

Meet of the hunt at Tretheague, c.1910 (from a postcard, Royal Institution of Cornwall).

Foundry as it was in the early 1900s. The gentleman standing on the left is Edwin Triggs. He and his wife had three sets of twins, two sets of girls and one set of boys, but sadly the boys died.

The Hare and the Hounds pub as it was in 1873 when Jethro Martin was the landlord. According to Kelly's Directory, there was a pub there from 1856. Foundry is a quiet residential area. During the 19th century there was a small foundry making Cornish shovels, a blacksmith's and a carpenter's shop and a factory making rope, run by the Peters family.

Above left: *The council houses in Collins Park, built on some small fields behind New Road where residents had previously kept their horses, their only means of transport. These were built in the early 1960s.*

Above: *Martins Terrace, just before it was demolished in the early 1960s. This was at the village end of Crellow Lane, then called Back Lane. There was another house on the end of the row where Miss Thomasine Vincent kept a sweet and tobacco shop. This was called Tammy's shop and the boys and girls used to tease and tantalise her unmercifully. People who lived in the houses included Miss Nora Way, Mrs Trerise and Morley, and Mrs Kemp who used to keep a chip shop (and who also made pasties for the schoolchildren in a large shed in the garden). Houses have now been built on the site.*

Left: *The Vineyard, the newest housing estate in Stithians, completed in 1999 by the Devon and Cornwall Housing Company for letting to eight families in Stithians.*

Right: *Deadmans Point between Longdowns and Rame Cross. There was a gin shop on the road near here early in the 19th century. On one occasion, whilst leaving the shop, a drunken party discovered that one among their number had a lot of money in his pocket. They stabbed him, dragged him to the top of the hill and he was found there next morning. He was buried there on the corner of the common at the junction with the road to Stithians. It was believed to be a case of 'felo de se' and burial in consecrated ground was therefore not permitted. This a story that has been handed down and was published in the* Eagle *magazine written by Samuel John Wills, schoolmaster at Wheal Ruby School, Wendron, in the late 1880s.*

Above: *An old picture of the Churchtown taken in the snow. The river runs down on the left before going under the road behind the houses on the right. The small wooden building on the end was used as a barber's shop. In the centre, you can just see the pump enclosed on three sides by a granite wall where the villagers pumped their water. Behind that is the entrance to Crellow House, and then the school.*

Left: *The other side of Back Lane as it used to be, with Mrs Susan Thomas standing outside.*

Right: *Half Moon House, in South Road, which was once a pub. In 1856 John Odgers was the landlord and in 1862 it was Joseph Odgers, in 1873 Miss Mary Martin, and in 1883 Willie Spargo. By 1902 it was a farm called Tremall run by a butcher and farmer listed in* Kelly's Directory *as one John Thomas Hellings.*

Top: *'Gunlaze' (Goonlaze) in the old days, before Mr Percy Williams' office was built and the cottages were rebuilt.*

Above: *Hendra Terrace built by the Martin family of Hendra House in the 1880s.*

Left: *The Post Office when it was at Hendra Terrace (with the postman, Dick Richards, outside).*

The rather splendid Trebarveth Farmhouse. Standing in front of the house is Ivan Day Perry, the farmer's son.

Another view of the village in the early 1900s. The girls on the right of the picture were the daughters of the butcher, Mr Richard James Opie, who lived there. The boy with crutches seems to be enjoying himself.

FAMILY GROCER & DRAPER,
MILLER, CORN & GENERAL
MERCHANT.
Telegrams: "PHILLIPS, STITHIANS."
Telephone: Perran-ar-Worthal
21-Y-6.
BOT. OF A. C. PHILLIPS
PENHALVEAN,
REDRUTH,
AND TRAVELLING SHOP
3
225

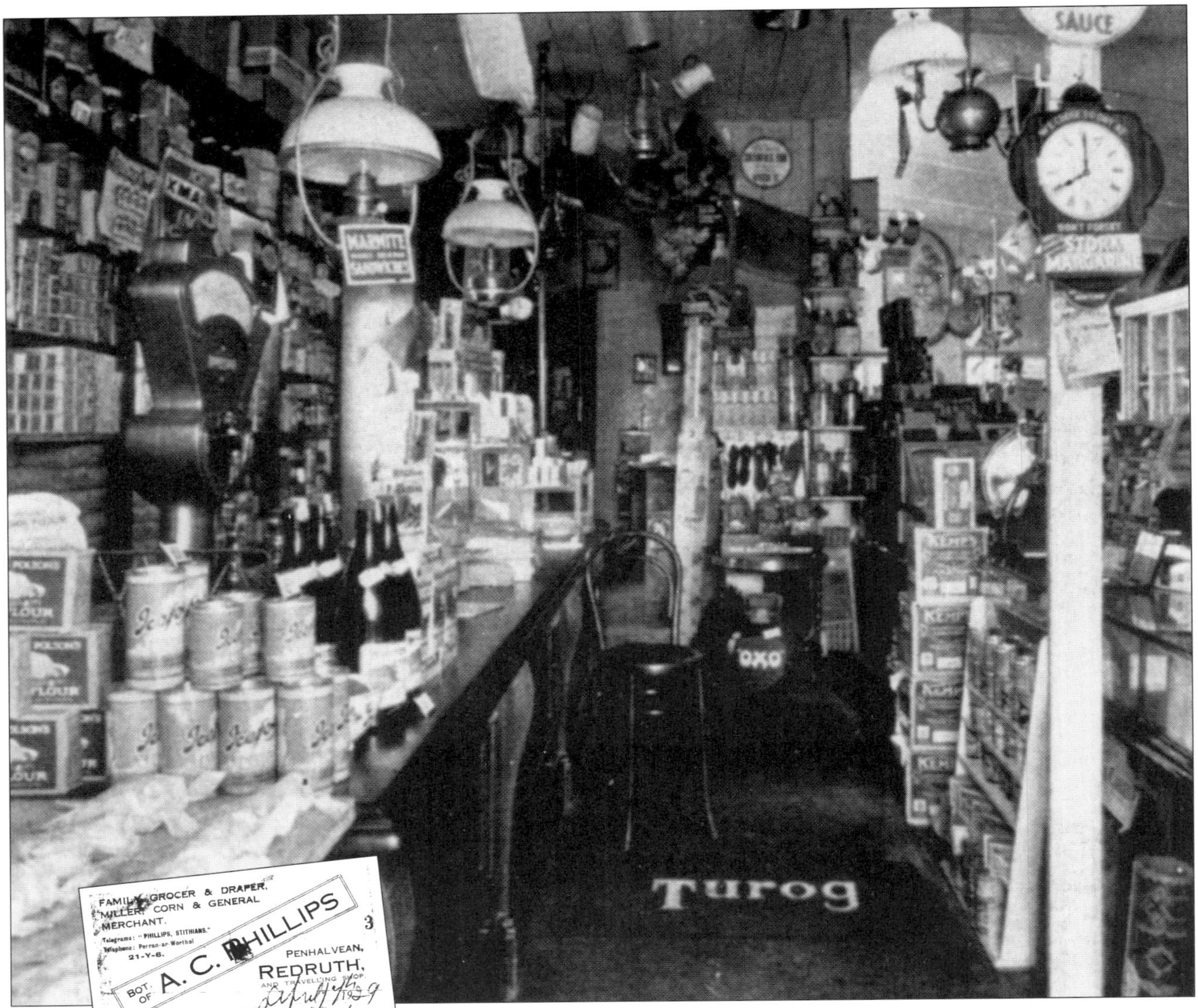

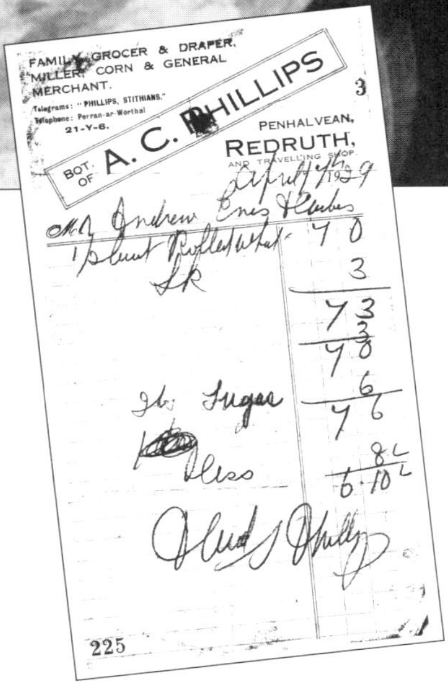

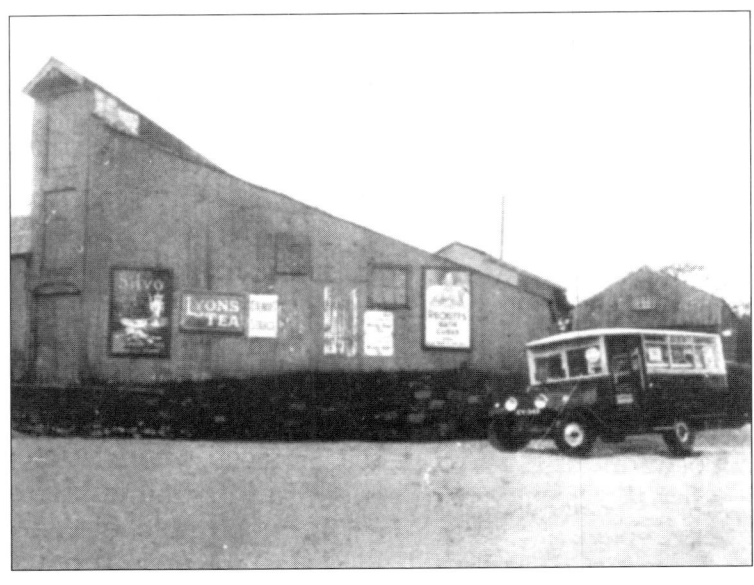

Above: *A.C. Phillips' shop interior, showing the scales, packets of yeast all weighed up on the counter, and a bent-wood chair for the customer to sit on whilst ordering goods. Everything that you can see was for sale.*

Left: *Bill-head for animal feed stuffs in 1929.*

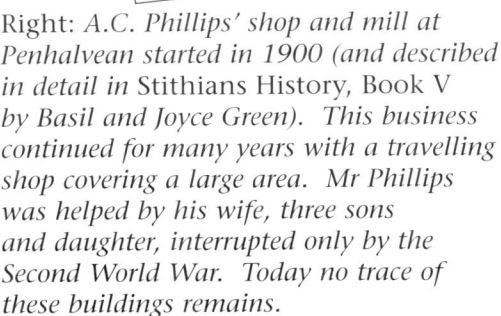

Right: *A.C. Phillips' shop and mill at Penhalvean started in 1900 (and described in detail in* Stithians History, Book V *by Basil and Joyce Green). This business continued for many years with a travelling shop covering a large area. Mr Phillips was helped by his wife, three sons and daughter, interrupted only by the Second World War. Today no trace of these buildings remains.*

Mr Phillips' travelling grocery van, a big six-cylinder Chevrolet fitted out with small shelves. Underneath there was a large storage tank for paraffin which people needed for fuel and light.

Above, main picture: *Longdowns village in the early 1900s with the blacksmith's shop on the right and the pub, the Stonemason's Arms, behind it, which has since been demolished. We know from Kelly's Directory that in 1862 James Opie was a beer retailer and a blacksmith there. The houses in the middle of the picture and the carpenter's shop were demolished when the road was widened. Note the one car and the horse and cart.*
Inset: *Aerial view of Longdowns taken in c.1960 just after a row of houses had been demolished on the left-hand side of the road (RNAS Culdrose).*

Sources
Written and Photographic

Books

Barton, D.B., *Essays in Cornish Mining History, Volume II*, 1970
Bates, Selina and Spurgin, Keith, *Stars in the Grass, the Life of Cornish Naturalist Frederick Hamilton Davey 1868-1915*, 1994
Bowden, Sydney J., *A Century of Music in Stithians, Book III*, 1984
Bowker, Alfred, *The King Alfred Millenary*
Cornish and Devon Granite Masters Association, *Handbook*, 1947
Council of St Stithians College and Mears, W.C.A., *The Early History of St Stithians College*, 1972
Cumber, W.G., *History of Stithians Church in Cornwall*
Daniell, Revd J.J., *A Geography of Cornwall*
Daniell, Revd J.J., *General History of Cornwall*, 1906
Davies, Gilbert Giddy, *The History of the Parishes of Cornwall*
Dickason, Graham B., *Cornish Immigrants to South Africa*, 1978
Douch, H.L, *Cornwall Muster Roll 1569*
Dunstan, C.D., *The Granite Industry in Stithians Parish*, 1967 (unpublished)
Earl, Bryan, MSc., *Cornish Explosives; The Trevithick Society*, 1978
Freeman, John and Company, *Cornish Granite*
Gasgoyne, Joel, *The Lanhydrock Atlas*
Gilbert, C.S., *County History, Volume II, Part II*, 1817
Gilbert, C.S., *History of Cornwall*, 1820
Gover, J.E.B., *Cornish Place Names MSS*
Hamilton Jenkin, A.K., *The Cornish Miner*, 1948
Hamilton Jenkin, A.K., *Mines and Miners of Cornwall, Volume VI*, 1981
Henderson, Charles, *Essays in Cornish History*, 1935
Henderson, Charles, *Sketch of the Manor of Penryn Corffe 1649-1758*
Hitchens and Drew, *The History of Cornwall*, 1824
Knuckey, Charles Kingscote (compil.), *130th Year Gathering of the Knuckey Family*
Lake, William, *The Complete Parochial History of Cornwall and General Armoury of the County 1872, Volume IV*
Martin, E.A., *A Cornish Community*, 1987
Martin, E.A., *The Martin Family of Stithians in Cornwall*, 1991
Martin, E.A., *Stithians Families, A Cornish Community*, 1987
Martin, E.A., *Stithians Families II*, 1998
Morrison, T.A., *Cornwall's Central Mines, The Southern District*, 1983
Penaluna, M.A., *Jane Hellings BEM, A Biography*, 1994
Penaluna, W., *Historical Survey of Sixty Parishes and Towns in Cornwall*
Pevsner, N., *Buildings of England*, 1970
Polwhele, R., *History of Cornwall*, 1816
Diaries of Richard Randall and John Randall Knuckey, S. Australia
Rogers, J.P., *Cornish Pedigrees*
Rowe, J.H. (edit), *Cornish Feet of Fines, Volume I*
Rowse, A.L., *Tudor Cornwall*, 1941
Spargo, John, *Verses Grave and Gay*, 1946
Stithians Parish History Group, *Always Something Interesting Vols I-IX* (Ed. Alison Penaluna)
Wallis, Christopher, *Journals*
Wills, Samuel J., *MSS Volume I*
Wills, Samuel J., *MSS Volume III*

Articles, Journals, Newspapers and Papers

Hants Chronicle (29 September 1951)
Henderson, Charles, 'Mount Edgecumbe Papers'
Kelly's Directories
National Savings Newsletter, December 1977
'Report to the Rt Hon. Secretary for State for the Home Department: No LXXXIII: Press House Kennall Vale 1888'
Royal Cornwall Gazette
Royal Cornwall Polytechnic Society, 'Annual Report', 1948
Royal Institution of Cornwall, 'Arundell Manor Survey'
Smith, John, R., Cornwall Trust for Nature Conservation, 'Kennall Vale Archaeological Report 1985-86: An Archaeological and Historical Study'
The *Star*, Johannesburg
Stithians Impounding Scheme
Stithians Joint Water Committee
Stoate, T.L., Cornwall Hearth and Poll Tax, 1660 and 1664
The *Stythian*
Stithians Times

Photography

Ascot Studio, Falmouth
Caddy, W.
Causey, Miss Alison
Cornish Studies Library
Cornwall County Council
Gleesons Civil Engineering Ltd.
Govier, S.J.
Green, Mrs Joyce A.
Hughes, H.
Hughes, Peter
Ivey, Mrs Janet C.M.
James, Derek
Lane, Mrs Belinda C.
Langford, Tony
Miles, John
Officer, Commanding, of the Royal Naval Air Station, Culdrose, Helston – James Derek
Penaluna, Mrs Alison
Phillips, Mrs E.M. (the late)
Roskrow, Robert
Roskrow, T.P.
Royal Institution of Cornwall
Society of Genealogists, London
Todd, David H. (the late),
Stithians Residents Association
The *West Briton*

Subscribers

Mrs J. Alsop, Southwick, Peterborough
Ken Andrew, Redruth, Cornwall
Mr & Mrs W. Andrew, Calgary, Canada
Valerie V. Andrew, Falmouth, Cornwall
Mrs M. Andrew, Penryn, Cornwall
Sylvia Andrew, Stithians, Cornwall
Bill Andrew, Calgary, Canada
K.A.C. Baker, Ponsanooth, Truro, Cornwall
J. & M. Balston, Stithians, Cornwall
Jayne & Simon Banner, Stithians, Cornwall
Mrs M. Barlow, Stithians, Cornwall
Pauline Barrett, Penponds, Camborne, Cornwall
Richard F. Bath, Melbourne, Australia
Joanna L. Bath, Brisbane, Australia
Capt. & Mrs G. W. Bazill, Ponsanooth, Truro, Cornwall
Mr R. W. Beal-King, Dorset
Richard J. Beale, Paignton, Devon
Rhoda Bennetts (née Triggs), Stithians, Cornwall
Mrs Benita Bernasconi, Geneva, Switzerland
Mrs S. K. Bettin, Stithians, Cornwall
Mrs D. Billinghurst, Whitstable, Kent
Mrs Julie A. Bingham, Stithians, Cornwall
Joan Biscoe, Truro, Cornwall
Dr & Mrs Biscoe, Stithians, Cornwall
Mr & Mrs B. Biscoe, Truro, Cornwall
James Alan Biscoe, Malawi
Charles Biscoe,
Joanna Biscoe,
Mr & Mrs A. Blake, Penzance, Cornwall
Clive & Elizabeth Bowden, Stithians, Cornwall
Lloyd J. Bradshaw, Victoria, Australia
Harold Brooks, Pelynt, Looe, Cornwall
Betty Brooks, Stithians, Cornwall
Doris K. Brown, Stithians, Cornwall
Marlene & Clyde Brush, Stithians, Cornwall
Jayne Brush & Robert May, Stithians, Cornwall
Ivor Bryant, formerly of Lanner, Cornwall
Margaret R. Bryant (née Bolitho), Mabe, Penryn, Cornwall
Jennifer & Peter Bullard, Stithians, Cornwall
Jack Burleigh, Stithians, Cornwall
Mr Des Burley, Stithians, Cornwall
Gloria E. Burley, St Day, Redruth, Cornwall
Laurie M. Burley, Penryn, Cornwall
Joan Butt, Banbury, Oxon
William & Marjorie Butt, Waltham Chase, Southampton
Jack Buzza (Family History Researcher), Truro, Cornwall
Daphne Campbell, Falmouth, Cornwall
Maureen Cannon, Bournemouth
J. C. Carbis (In-Pensioner), Chelsea, London
Rosemary Chamberlain, Penryn, Cornwall
Michael J. Charles, Leeds
Mrs Veronica Chesher M.A., B. LITT., East Looe, Cornwall
Mr J. Cole, Stithians, Cornwall
Mavis & Eric Collins, Perranarworthal, Cornwall
Jane Corey B.Sc., formerly of Carncrees, Stithians, Cornwall
Annoula Couldry, Stithians, Cornwall
Mrs Jane Craven (née Opie), Stithians, Cornwall
Lynne & Phil Crook, Stithians, Cornwall
Mrs P. M. Dale, Gwennap, Redruth, Cornwall
Hilda Davis (née Paull), Lutterworth, Leics.
William R. J. Dingle, Swansea, Tasmania, Australia
I. R. Downing, Seureaugh Farm, Stithians, Cornwall
Miss D. Downing, Falmouth, Cornwall
Geoffrey & Velma Downing, Chacewater, Truro, Cornwall
Mr & Mrs K. R. Downing, Stithians, Cornwall
W. V. Duck (née Sarah), Upton-by-Chester, Cheshire
Denman Dunstan, Falmouth, Cornwall
Sharon & Nigel Dunstan, Stithians, Cornwall
Miss. W. P. Dunstan, Kenwyn Hill, Truro, Cornwall
David Dunstan, Reading, Berkshire
Christopher D. Dunstan, Crediton, Devon
Ruth & Reg Dunstan, Stithians, Cornwall
Dr Francis E. Dunstan, High Wycombe, Bucks
Mr F. J. Dunstan, Redruth, Cornwall
Ron F. Dunstan, Eastcote, Ruislip, Middlesex
Jeffrey F. Dunstan, Melbourne, Australia
Kathleen Dunstan, Stithians, Cornwall
Tony Elliott, Stithians, Cornwall
Louise Ely, Palmers Green, London N13
Mr Noel & Mrs Joyce Ford, Pelynt, Looe, Cornwall
Louie V. Ford, Stithians, Cornwall
Mrs Dorothy Francis, Stithians, Cornwall
W. Russell Gay, Truro, Cornwall
Canon Michael B. Geach, Truro, Cornwall
The George family, Stithians, Cornwall
Mr G. R. Gibson, Waitara, New South Wales, Australia
Clara Gill (née Triggs), Stithians, Cornwall
Mr J. R. Glennie, Connor Downs, Hayle, Cornwall
Paul & Jean Gluyas, Stithians, Cornwall

Phyllis Gluyas, Stithians, Cornwall
Mrs Olive Gluyas, Stithians, Cornwall
Paul & Rachel Godwin, Stithians, Cornwall
David Green, Rosemanowes, Stithians, Cornwall
Andrew & Lyn Green, Exeter, Devon
Mrs K. G. Greenwood, Broadstairs, Kent
Laura Jane Groves, Stithians, Cornwall
W. Joan Haynes (née Opie), Exmouth, Devon
Alfred S. Hearn, Perth, Australia (formerly of Stithians)
Richard & Carol Heginbotham, Solihull, West Midlands
J. Heywood, Stithians, Cornwall
Sue Higgens (née Knuckey), Tunstall, Woodbridge, Suffolk
Kim V. Hill, Stithians, Cornwall
Barbara A. Hill, California, USA
Brian P. Hooper, Goonlaze, Stithians, Cornwall
K. M. Hosken, Camborne, Cornwall
James-Carol Ivey, Truro, (formerly of Stithians)
David Jarvis, Carnkie, Cornwall
Margery Jellie, Menherion, Redruth, Cornwall
Jacqueline Jenkins, Stithians, Cornwall
David Jenkins, Stithians, Cornwall
Chrissie Jenkins (née Triggs), Stithians, Cornwall
Desmond Joyce, Poole, Dorset
Annie Van Kleeff (née Corey), Stithians, Cornwall
Hugh Kneebone, Perranwell Station, Truro, Cornwall
Dudley W. F. Kneebone, Perranwell, (formerly of Stithians), Cornwall
Major & Mrs T. S. Knipe (née Knuckey), Reading, Berkshire
John R. Knuckey, Ponsanooth, Truro, Cornwall
R. Gordon Knuckey, Melbourne, Australia
Vernon Victor Knuckey, Mulwala, NSW, Australia
Mrs J. Lamerton, Penryn, Cornwall
Melanie Jane & Ryan A. C. Lane, Weston-Super-Mare
Christopher D. J. Lane, Lipson, Plymouth, Devon
Mr & Mrs M. A. Lane, Emerson's Green, Bristol
Mrs Glencoe Langford, Redruth, Cornwall
Roger J. Langford, Redruth, Cornwall
Rosamund Lawrance, Stithians, Cornwall
Lee family, Anghering Village, Sussex
Mr & Mrs F. J. Lennox Green, Penzance, Cornwall
Paul Propert Lewis, Stithians, Cornwall
Muriel & Jim Liddle, Stithians, Cornwall
Mr & Mrs D. Lidgett, Hertingfordbury, Herts.
Catherine Lorigan, Delabole
Mr & Mrs W. Lovell, Ealing, London
Mrs M. Luxton, Lower Compton, Plymouth, Devon
Rex Manhire, Illogan, Redruth, Cornwall
Robert Marron, Stithians, Cornwall
Eric J. Martin, Stithians, Cornwall
Keith Martin, Stithians, Cornwall
Tony & Mary Martin, Stithians, Cornwall
Stuart Hearle Martin, Warradale, South Australia
William R. Martin, Geelong, Australia
Edward Martin, Hitcham, Suffolk
Mr Dudley Martin (Trebowling ancestors), Childers, Queensland, Australia
Mrs Gussie Matteson, Stithians, Cornwall
Tamsin Louise Mead, Stithians, Cornwall
Carol & Glynn Mitchell, Foundry, Stithians, Cornwall
Mrs P. Monger, Cheriton Bishop, Exeter, Devon
Merle D. Moyle, Stithians, Cornwall
Ian & Sheila Moyle, Menerdue, Redruth, Cornwall
Edward R. Murphy, formerly of Stithians, Cornwall
Nicholls family, Trevales Farm, Stithians, Cornwall
Dr Norman D. Nicol, USA
Leila M. Odgers, Redruth, Cornwall
Mrs E. Offord, Falmouth, Cornwall
William & Betty Oliver, The Homestead, Trevarth, Lanner, Cornwall
John Olson, Stithians, Cornwall
Colin Opie, Ottery St Mary, Devon
Karen D. J. Oppy, Longdowns, Penryn, Cornwall
Gwen Oulds, Ilford, Essex/ formerly Stithians, Cornwall
Mrs Betty Paget, Stithians, Cornwall
Roger Parker, Lanner, Cornwall
Mrs Heather Parker, Southampton
Mr Dennis G. Parsons, Romford, Essex (formerly of Stithians)
Rex & Peggy Pascoe, Stithians, Cornwall
Mollie & Mervyn Pascoe, Stithians, Cornwall
Amy J. Pascoe, Stithians, Cornwall
Ron R. Pascoe, Colchester, Essex
Mrs B. Nancy Pearce, Stithians, Cornwall
Mrs Marion Penaluna, Crellow Hill, Stithians, Cornwall
Mr & Mrs E. Penlerick, Menherion, Redruth, Cornwall
Mr & Mrs John Penna, Tregew Barton, Truro, Cornwall
Dominick Penrose, Stithians, Cornwall
Edward (Ted) Perry, Surrey (formerly Stithians)
Mr Ivan D. Perry, Helston, Cornwall
Mr R. C. Phillips, Stithians, Cornwall
Mr Charles & Mrs Sallie Phillips, Illogan, Redruth, Cornwall
Peter W. Phillips, Stithians, Cornwall
Sarah E. Pike, Stithians, Cornwall
Simon J. W. Pike, Stithians, Cornwall
T. K. Plummer, Truro, Cornwall
J. Neil Plummer (Bath), An Velyn Seaureaugh, St. Stithians, Kernow, Cornwall

SUBSCRIBERS

Malcolm & Ros Pochon, Lower Durian, Stithians, Cornwall
John B. Porter, Hurstpierpoint, West Sussex
Mrs Pauline Potts, Stithians, Cornwall
Phil Preen, Stithians, Cornwall
John C. C. Probert, Redruth, Cornwall
M. Joyce Prowse, Summercourt, Newquay, Cornwall
Wilfred Brian Prowse, Stithians, Cornwall
Edgar J. Pryor, Stithians, Cornwall
Vivian Pryor, Newquay, Cornwall
Anne & Jeff Purkis, Penhalvean, Redruth, Cornwall
Anthony Graham Rackstraw, Timaru, New Zealand
Margaret Ramsey, Stithians, Cornwall
David H. Rayner, Stithians, Cornwall
Roger J. Reay, Foundry, Stithians, Cornwall
Michael C. Reed, Bristol
Ann E. Reed, Portishead, Bristol
Lester & Margaret Reed, Portishead, Bristol
Mr Jack Reed, Winchester, Hants.
R. D. Reed, Chipping Norton, Oxon
Brian Reed, Redruth, Cornwall
Mr & Mrs S. Relton, Stithians, Cornwall
Miss Susannah Relton, Stithians, Cornwall
Mr K. F. Richards, Weston-Super-Mare, Somerset
Dr E. T. E. Richards, Penzance, Cornwall
Paul Richards, Brea
Ian & Laura Richards, Little Mill, Stithians, Cornwall
M. Robertson, Stithians, Cornwall
Ethel May Rowe, Truro, Cornwall
Dom. Joseph Roy Sarah O.S.B., Buckfast Abbey, Devon
Noel & Margaret Shaw, Victoria, Australia
Ian Shaw, Stithians, Cornwall
Ray Smith, Cowper Road, Peterborough
Bill & Betty Smith, Fairlawns, Stithians, Cornwall
Sarah K. Smith, Stithians, Cornwall
Mr & Mrs James Smith & daughters, Stithians, Cornwall
Angeline & Ken Sowden, Constantine, Cornwall
Gary T. Spargo, Texas, USA
Charles Spicer, Carnon Downs, Truro, Cornwall
David & Daya Stafford, Stithians, Cornwall
William (Billy) Stapleton, Falmouth, Cornwall
Stithians County Primrary School, Cornwall
Olive Stribley, Stithians, Cornwall
Lucy M. Swan (née Triggs), Stithians, Cornwall
Eleanor M. Symons, Playing Place
Lynn Thomas, Stithians, Cornwall
Joe Thomas, Illogan, Redruth, Cornwall
Mr Michael D. Thomas, Falmouth, Cornwall
Vyvyan, Yvonne & Bryher Toms, Stithians, Cornwall
Neil Trerise, Stithians, Cornwall
Carl Trerise,
Mr & Mrs Grenville Tresidder, Crellow Lane, Stithians, Cornwall
Martin Trispen, Truro, Cornwall
Mrs Yvonne Truen, Penryn, Cornwall
Mrs E. M. Ungerson, Stithians, Cornwall
Mr & Mrs J. N. J. Usoro, Stithians, Cornwall
Caroline Veall, Stithians, Cornwall
Mrs Joy Walker (née Penaluna), formerly of Carncrees, Stithians, Cornwall
W. E. Walley, Ponsanooth, Truro, Cornwall
Canon Michael & Mrs Rosemary Warner, Tregony, Truro, Cornwall
Geoff Warren, New South Wales, Australia
Mrs M. Waters, Cowlands Creek, Truro, Cornwall
Mr & Mrs S. A. Watters, Stithians, Cornwall
Hugh Webb, Stithians, Cornwall
Mr C. N. Wiblin, Shrewton, Salisbury, Wiltshire
J. Larry Williams, Hope, USA
Joyce L. Williams, Plymouth, Devon
Enid A. Williams, Plymouth, Devon
Mrs D. F. Williams, Gorran, St Austell, Cornwall
Mrs E. M. Williams, Treskewes, Stithians, Cornwall
F. Julian Williams, Caerhays Castle, Veryan, Cornwall
Jill & Leonard Williams, Arwenack Manor, Falmouth, Cornwall
Mr & Mrs W. Williams, Stithians, Cornwall
Inez M. Williams, Redruth, Cornwall
Mary C. Williams, Stithians, Cornwall
Trevor Wills, Warwick
Ros Wills, Taunton, Somerset
Anne Wilson, Deniliquin, New South Wales, Australia
Ashley Wood, Penhalveor, Redruth, Cornwall
Stephen & Rita Wood, Stithians, Cornwall
Sheila Mary Wrench (née James), Caversham, Berkshire
D. B. Wylde - Rector, St. Stithians College, South Africa
Jean Young, Illogan, Cornwall

THE BOOK OF STITHIANS

Also available in the Community History Series:
The Book of Bampton Caroline Seward
Clearbrook, The Story of a Dartmoor Hamlet Pauline Hemery
The Book of Cornwood and Lutton, Photographs and Reminiscences compiled by the People of the Parish
The Ellacombe Book Sydney R. Langmead
The Book of Lamerton, A Photographic History Ann Cole and Friends
Lanner – A Cornish Mining Parish Sharron Schwartz and Roger Parker
The Book of Grampound with Creed Amy Bane and Mary Oliver
The Book of Manaton
The Book of Meavy Pauline Hemery
The Book of Morchard Bishop Jeff Kingaby
The Book of North Newton J.C. Robins and K.C. Robins
The Book of Plymtree, The Parish and Its People compiled and edited by Tony Eames
The Book of Porlock Dennis Corner
Postbridge –The Heart of Dartmoor Reg Bellamy
The Book of Torbay, A Century of Celebration Frank Pearce
The Book of Trusham Alick Cameron
Widecombe–in–the–Moor Stephen Woods
Woodbury, The Twentieth Century Revisited compiled by Roger Stokes

Forthcoming titles in the Community History Series:
The Book of Chittlehampton
The Book of Bickington Stuart Hands
The Book of Bickleigh
The Book of Helston Derek Carter
The Book of Ilsington Dick Wills
The Lustleigh Book
The Book of Lyndhurst Roy Jackman
The Book of Meneage Derek Carter
The Book of Silverton Graham Parnell
The Book of South Tawton and South Zeal Roy and Ursula Radford

Further information:
If you would like to order a book or find out more about having your parish featured in this series, please contact The Editor, Community History Series, Halsgrove House, Lower Moor Way, Tiverton Business Park, Tiverton, Devon, EX16 6SS, tel: 01884 243242 or visit us at http://www.halsgrove.com
If you are interested in a particular photograph in this volume, it may be possible to supply you with a copy of the image.

Mrs E.K. Andrew on Ambella Bridge just before the land was flooded for the reservoir. She is remembering the time she and her husband farmed Ambella Farm (1914-1923).